DIVE INTO
Close
Reading

Complexity Chunk
Text-dependent
Guided
Scaffold Tone
Assessment Reread
Underline
Details Craft
Question Vocabulary
Partner Discuss Annotate
Structure
Connections Point of View

Diane Lapp, Ed.D., Barbara Moss, Ph.D.,
Maria Grant, Ph.D., and Kelly Johnson, Ed.D.

Foreword by Lori Oczkus, M.A.

Contributing Authors

Stephanie Herweck Rice
Jodene Smith, M.A.

Publishing Credits

Corinne Burton, M.A.Ed., *President*
Conni Medina, M.A.Ed., *Managing Editor*
Nika Fabienke, Ed.D., *Content Director*
Emily R. Smith, M.A.Ed., *Project Consultant*
Sara Johnson, M.S.Ed., *Project Consultant*
Monique Dominguez, *Graphic Designer*
Valerie Morales, *Assistant Editor*

Image Credits

p.162 illustration by Timothy J. Bradley; all other images iStock and/or Shutterstock.

Standards

Shell Education

A division of Teacher Created Materials
5301 Oceanus Drive
Huntington Beach, CA 92649-1030

www.tcmpub.com/shell-education
ISBN 978-1-4258-1540-0
©2017 Shell Education Publishing, Inc.

Table of Contents

Acknowledgments 4

Foreword 5

Section 1: Close Reading Introduced 7

Section 2: Planning Close Reading 19

Section 3: Teaching Close Reading 52

Section 4: Assessing and Extending Close Reading 64

Section 5: Literary Text Close Reading Lessons 76

Section 6: Informational Text Close Reading Lessons 169

References Cited 263

Glossary of Reteaching Ideas 264

Contents of the Digital Download 267

Acknowledgments

We want to acknowledge all the teachers who believe that being literate is the inalienable right of every student. Their daily instructional actions indicate their actualization of this right.

We also want to thank Sara Johnson for her initial belief in this program and Kristina Mazaika, Emily Smith, and Nika Fabienke who shepherded it to the finish line. We appreciate each of you.

Diane, Barbara, Maria, and Kelly

Foreword

At last, close reading is demystified and made practical in this fabulous resource, put together by the respected team of Diane Lapp, Barbara Moss, Maria Grant, and Kelly Johnson! The authors bring their rich classroom experiences and knowledge of the reading process to this useful tool, designed especially for grades K–2. The movie title of *Dive into Close Reading: Strategies for Your K–2 Classroom* could be *Everything You Wanted to Know About Close Reading But Were Afraid to Ask!* Whether you already teach students to read closely or are new to the term, *Dive into Close Reading* is for you! This useful and classroom-tested resource is jam-packed with grade specific ideas and detailed lesson samples to use all year long. Whether you read *Dive into Close Reading* on your own or if you study close reading in a professional learning community in your school or district, this is a wonderful book!

In my work around the country as a literacy consultant, I find that the definition of *close reading* varies as well as the practices related to it. The authors of this text aptly define close reading as an approach for all students to develop deep comprehension of complex texts, including English language learners and below-level readers. They add that, "In close reading, students act as investigators, gradually uncovering the meaning of short pieces of literature or informational texts. Through the process of reading, questioning, focusing, and rereading the texts, students uncover the 'bones' or main ideas of the passage." The authors claim that rereading to delve deeper into texts is at the heart of close reading.

Today, teachers still ask lots of questions regarding the implementation of close reading and what models work best. The authors of *Dive into Close Reading* address the issues and problems teachers share when incorporating quality close reading lessons in their classrooms. Here are some of the current concerns teachers may express with close reading:

- What is the definition of close reading?
- How can I make close reading relevant to my students so that they will do it on their own?
- What types of texts, including complex texts, should I use in my lessons?
- What are some ways to motivate students to reread during close reading lessons?
- How can I teach close reading using the materials I already have in my classroom?
- What are some lesson formats that fit different types of texts and genres?
- What is the most effective use of text-dependent questions during lessons?
- How can I make time for close reading?
- How does close reading differ from other familiar reading approaches?
- What is the best way to teach students to annotate text?
- How can I use close reading to promote better comprehension and critical thinking?

Dive into Close Reading is not only chock-full of research-based how-to questions and answers, but also includes sample texts and lessons that engage students in the close reading process. Teachers will welcome the easy-to-read format and concrete examples. *Dive into Close Reading* has a unique format that is really a two-in-one professional book, plus a rich sample lesson treasure trove. The authors have taken the guesswork out of creating close reading lesson plans that really work!

Dive into Close Reading features:

→ Rubrics for evaluating texts based on:
- what the text says
- how the text works
- what the text means

→ Grade-specific text-dependent questions charts for grades K–2 that teachers will want to use every day!

→ Suggestions for scaffolding tools, such as partner texts, realia, or illustrations.

→ Concrete ideas for performance tasks that are grade-level specific. For example, in kindergarten, coloring in key items in an illustration; or in 1st grade, drawing the perfect dog park; or in 2nd grade, writing a letter about how to play safely.

→ Concrete strategies for helping struggling readers and English language learners grasp concepts.

→ Very specific sample lesson plans and strategies for literary texts for each grade level K–2.

→ Very specific sample lesson plans and strategies for informational texts for each grade level K–2.

Join me in congratulating authors Diane Lapp, Barbara Moss, Maria Grant, and Kelly Johnson for their brilliant exploration of close reading and their generous gift of a practical guide to illustrate the approach. Every teacher will want a copy on their desks to use all year long as they help students *Dive into Close Reading*!

—Lori Oczkus

Literacy Consultant and Coauthor of the
Close Reading with Paired Texts K–5 series

Section 1:
Close Reading Introduced

A Short Scenario

In Mrs. Mohr's first grade classroom, students are studying animal environments. To begin the unit, Mrs. Mohr selects a section from the text *A Visit to a Farm*, by D. M. Rice, to use for a close reading. The text tells the story of a family's visit to a farm and embeds information about animals through words and photographs. Take a look at this sample page of text.

> Next, we saw the horse corral. There were horses and ponies standing nose to nose. They looked like they were talking to each other.

This paragraph includes science language (corral, horses, ponies), general language (next, standing), and a comprehension challenge (noticing that the horses *looked* like they were talking to each other, but were not actually talking to each other). How can a teacher guide students to notice and comprehend the important details of a text with increasing independence? That's the question asked by thousands of teachers as they sit down to craft meaningful lessons that involve reading complex texts.

Fortunately, there is an answer to this question—an effective, thoughtful, research-based means of implementing close reading that can be personalized to meet the needs of any teacher's students. The key is to guide students to unlock meaning through strategically crafted, text-dependent questions.

Let us return to Mrs. Mohr's first grade class to see how she does this.

Mrs. Mohr begins by reading the paragraph with the students and asking them to think about the question, "What's this about?" Students are instructed to return to the displayed text guide to underline key words and ideas.

First graders Livi and Min feel confident in their annotation skills. They have practiced with Mrs. Mohr for months now. Following the teacher's first read and class annotation, students pair up to read individual copies of the text. They chat with partners and share their thoughts. Mrs. Mohr directs them by saying, "Reread the text to answer the question, *What details help you understand the text?*"

Annotation markings: marks a reader adds to a text to record his or her thinking. For more information about annotations, see Table 3.2 on pages 58–59.

Annotation statements: spoken form of annotation marks. Students who are not yet fluent writers can speak or dictate their thinking about the text.

Annotation gestures: physical form of annotation marks. Students who are not yet fluent writers and speakers can point, mime, or nod to express their thinking about the text.

Livi: I think it's about horses.

Min: Yeah, they went to see the horses. And what's this word? [Points to *corral*.]

Livi: I don't know. Let's circle it.

Min: Let's ask Mrs. Mohr to read the sentence. [To Mrs. Mohr] Can you help us read this sentence?

Mrs. Mohr, Livi, and Min (reading): Next, we saw the horse corral.

Livi: Oh, it's the horse area. Right?

Min: Yeah, they went to the barn. Then they went to the horse area.

Mrs. Mohr: What clues does the picture provide to help you understand the important words in the sentences?

Min: It shows what the horse area is like.

Livi: Yeah, the corral.

Min: It has grass.

Livi: A fence.

Mrs. Mohr uses student annotations and partner talk to guide her next steps. She offers appropriate text-dependent questions to help students unlock meaning for themselves. She guides students by strategically directing their attention to specific areas in the text and supporting graphics. In doing so, she empowers them to use their insights and those gained from conversing with their peers. Her instruction includes close assessment of student performance, fostering independence, and building self-esteem. This is evident as Livi and Min continue to talk after Mrs. Mohr's questioning.

Min: It says they look like they are talking to each other. But horses can't talk.

Livi: Right. In the picture, they're close together.

Min: And it says nose to nose.

Livi: I think they are being friends. They look like they are talking to each other, but they are really just standing together to be friends.

Min: Right. Let's say that to the class.

Livi: Let's tell them about corral, too.

As this scenario illustrates, students begin to feel capable when they learn to read complex texts on their own, which is a teacher's dream. This book serves as a guide to teachers as they follow Mrs. Mohr's lead—teachers like you, who are teaching students to closely read complex texts by challenging them with appropriate text-dependent questions that build reading skills, deepen comprehension, and foster independence.

The Close Reading Approach

Compare today's modern, dynamic classrooms to the educational system from 50 years ago, and it is obvious that huge improvements have been made in the teaching profession. As a frontline educator, you have never before been so well positioned to serve the ever-evolving needs of an increasingly diverse student body, but there are still areas that need attention. Every year, new techniques and buzzwords swirl around, each one promising to open the world of knowledge and critical thought to students. Some live up to their promises, and some fizzle, only to be replaced by the next big thing the following year. You must carefully evaluate new techniques to ensure that they will be of actual benefit to students. No one denies that students need strong preparation for future careers and college. The question is, and always has been, *how* can we best provide students with the skills they need to lead productive, successful lives? The close reading approach described in this book is a terrific place to start.

Close reading is a powerful, useful, and successful approach for teaching reading comprehension and critical-thinking skills. The lessons and strategies described in this book have been piloted and refined by classroom teachers, are backed by current pedagogical research, and are aligned with college and career readiness standards from around the country. Using the close reading approach simply means building upon current practices. Table 1.1 lists useful definitions for terms used in the close reading approach.

Table 1.1 Useful Definitions for the Close Reading Approach

Term	Working Definition
annotation	the process of marking a text with information and questions for further study; may include highlights, symbols, notes, and comments
chunking	dividing a text into smaller pieces, or chunks, numbered for ease of reference and study
close thinking	a sister approach to close reading, where students think deeply about texts that are read aloud to them, as opposed to texts they are reading independently; especially useful technique with early readers who do not yet have the decoding skills necessary to tackle a particular text
guided reading	a small-group reading approach in which a teacher supports developing readers through individualized scaffolding; a segment of a balanced literacy program designed to support students, growing independence as readers
qualitative	unable to be defined numerically; factors include things such as student background knowledge with a topic, author purpose, and language features

Table 1.1 Useful Definitions for the Close Reading Approach *(cont.)*

Term	Working Definition
quantitative	can be defined and assessed numerically, such as by grade level, number of words per page, and word length
scaffold	support for a student's learning; a tailored teaching practice used with the intent of helping the student achieve his or her learning goals
shared reading	an interactive reading experience in which the teacher models the skills of a fluent reader
text-dependent question (TDQ)	a question that is based on the text itself rather than personal experiences and can only be answered by someone who has read a particular text selection
text complexity	a measure of the level of challenge presented by a particular text selection for a student at a given grade level
thinking aloud	technique of speaking the thoughts that occur while reading; a process that can be used to model or assess a particular skill

Frequently Asked Questions

What does the close reading of complex texts really mean?

When a fluent reader approaches a text, he or she does more than simply decode the words. The fluent reader begins by wondering: *What do I know about this? Who wrote this? What do I know about that person? When was it written? Is this a book, a pamphlet, an excerpt, a magazine article, a newspaper article, an advertisement, or some other kind of writing? What sort of font is being used, and what does that imply about the writing?* Once the reading begins, this mental questioning process continues, and the reader looks for answers within the text. The fluent reader may reread sections or, if the selection is very short, an entire passage, as understanding of the piece evolves. A truly rich and complex text may be revisited many times over a lifetime, with the reader making new and interesting discoveries with each rereading.

Close reading is a structured approach that enables all students, including English language learners and students reading below grade level, to develop deep comprehension of complex grade-level texts. In close reading, students act as investigators, gradually uncovering the meaning of short pieces of literature or informational texts. Through the process of reading, questioning, focusing, and rereading the texts, students uncover the "bones" or main ideas of the passage. Students return again and again to the text, becoming ever more adept at identifying and interacting with the language, context, structure, and layers of embedded meaning. This emphasis on repeatedly returning to the same text to gradually acquire a comfortable and deep understanding is at the heart of the close reading approach.

Why do today's standards require the close reading of complex texts?

Comprehension of complex texts is linked to success on high-stakes assessments of college and career readiness and to actual success in college and career. Today's standards require instruction and supported practice with close reading of complex texts.

A study by the college readiness testing company, ACT (2006), evaluated the results of 568,000 ACT reading tests taken by eighth, tenth, and twelfth grade students. These test results were compared with a benchmark level of "college readiness," a standard meant to predict college acceptance, retention, and the achievement of a 3.0 GPA. Next, the researchers analyzed the student responses with the goal of identifying which factors were indicative of success. Students who were able to read and

> The Partnership for Assessment of Readiness for College and Careers determined that "a significant body of research links the close reading of complex texts—whether the student is a struggling reader or advanced—to significant gains in reading proficiency and finds close reading to be a key component of college and career readiness." (2011, 7)

comprehend the most complex texts were the ones most likely to have high scores on the college-readiness standard. The ACT researchers found that, "Students who can read complex texts are more likely to be ready for college. Those who cannot read complex texts are less likely to be ready for college" (2005, 5).

Additionally, there is currently a significant difference between the complexity of texts being used at the twelfth grade level and those being utilized in career and college settings. In his 2006 study, Gary L. Williamson reported that there is a gap greater than 1.5 standard deviations between the levels of these texts, a larger difference than that between typical fourth and eighth grade texts!

At what grade level should we begin using the close reading approach?

Today's reading standards require students of all ages to engage in a much more critical analysis of the texts they read. The earlier students begin to closely read, the better able they are to read increasingly complex texts. The close reading approach should be introduced to even the youngest readers. In this way, close reading will become a habit of mind when tackling challenging texts (Boyles 2012). Emphasizing the need to repeatedly return to a text in order to uncover evidence for perceived meaning is an essential skill which can and should be applied in all areas of academic study. Introducing this concept as early as possible can improve students' academic performance throughout their careers.

How does close reading work with beginning readers?

College and Career Readiness standards require that first graders be able to comprehend complex literature and informational texts with prompting and support. By second grade, students must comprehend complex texts with supports as needed. Thus, at the early grade levels, when students may not have the foundational decoding skills necessary to engage in fully independent reading, they are expected to receive structured assistance in reaching their reading goals. With younger students, the close reading techniques in this book may include a more scaffolded approach. The teacher may do the reading as the students engage in close thinking. Students should be encouraged to participate in *close thinking*, by making mental annotations as the teacher reads aloud. The same sort of questioning, deeply critical analysis, and revisiting of the text will occur, but with the prompting, guidance, and modeling of a proficient teacher ready to assist with the foundational elements.

Why should close reading replace tried-and-true reading approaches?

It shouldn't! There is nothing about close reading that precludes the use of other approaches that work well for you and your students. You can and should continue to use successful approaches, such as guided reading, shared reading, book study, and collaborative groups. Close reading is an approach that will support your students in deeply and critically analyzing all types of complex texts. It is not meant to be the sole approach or strategy for literacy development in your classroom. Think of it as an additional, powerful tool in your teaching toolbox. As every craftsperson knows, it is important to use the right tool for each job. The close reading tool is exceptionally useful when teaching students how to approach, analyze, and deeply connect with complex literature and informational texts.

How does close reading differ from other familiar reading approaches?

Close reading focuses on short, complex texts or self-contained sections of texts that are revisited multiple times. Before the reading, teachers *do not frontload information* for students. Unlike guided, shared, or read-aloud sessions, it is not recommended that teachers model skills and strategies or preteach background information before students read or listen to a text during the close reading. There is, however, nothing to preclude a teacher from inviting students to closely read a subsection of a text or a stanza of a poem that is already under study or that has been previously shared as a read aloud. However, during the actual close reading, students are encouraged to independently *have a go* at a text selected for its complexity and placement in their appropriate Lexile band. During the first reading, students should read or listen to uncover the big ideas and key details of the text. Students engage in repeated readings of the text to access deeper meaning, including how the text works, by scrutinizing the author's craft and the meaning of the text. Student annotations should illustrate their thinking, as well as their points of confusion, any unknown vocabulary, and other questions or points of interest they wish to pursue more deeply.

At every juncture, the main role of the teacher is to assess students' performance and provide scaffolds to support their text analysis. This happens, for example, while listening in on conversations to determine the direction to take in the next read, identifying the next questions to ask to push students deeper into the analysis of the text during the next read, and reassessing student needs. The major scaffold teachers provide is through the continuous questions they ask: *What does the text say? What evidence can you find for that? How is the information conveyed? Can you find that in the text?* Purposeful questions help students resolve the complexity and uniqueness of each text.

Close reading preplanning is essential. Preplanning of text-dependent questions is a must for the success of a close reading lesson. Unlike other instructional reading approaches, however, close reading cannot be completely preplanned. Although you may craft an initial set of questions before students begin reading the text, tailoring questions and dialogue to the issues and questions that arise during students' reading is powerful and authentic. Close reading experiences occur organically and can never be recreated. Each encounter with the text should, however, push students to deeper levels of understanding.

What do I do after a close read?

Close reading experiences should conclude with performance tasks that encourage students to demonstrate their learning. These tasks may include writing, slide shows, reader's theater, art projects, or any other activity designed to further extend students' learning and provide them with an opportunity to share their mastery of the learning goals for the lesson. If students are still struggling or unable to competently demonstrate their knowledge, reteaching may be in order. See pages 264–266 for assessment and reteaching ideas.

Close Reading Management

The easiest way to manage the scheduling of close reading is to encompass other literacy practices within the close reading session. For example, if you use shared reading regularly, try using a close reading approach involving a shared reading component. Similarly, close reading can be easily rotated into your guided reading lessons. As students' proficiency with close reading increases, it becomes easier to incorporate it throughout your curriculum.

Generally, we believe that students should have opportunities to engage in close reading on a daily basis. However, these experiences should ideally be spread across all areas of study, not just with specified language arts lessons. A student might engage in close reading for a math lesson on Monday, a social studies lesson on Tuesday, and a language arts lesson on Wednesday. It is essential that students have ample opportunities to make close reading a deeply ingrained habit so that they can depend on these skills to propel them beyond surface reading for the rest of their lives.

The close reading approach is structured for whole-group instruction and partner work. However, when students struggle, small-group scaffolding becomes necessary. In those cases, a small group can be pulled together while the rest of the students are engaged in independent or small-group work that does not require teacher attention. Table 1.2 illustrates how one teacher incorporated close reading in her classroom over the course of a week.

Table 1.2 Incorporating Close Reading

Content Area	Monday	Tuesday	Wednesday	Thursday	Friday
Language Arts	(close reading:) *Tom Sawyer* pp. 40–41	read aloud: *Tom Sawyer* chapter 5	(close reading:) *Tom Sawyer* p. 101	read aloud: *Tom Sawyer* chapter 6	read aloud: *Tom Sawyer* chapter 7
Science	lecture and shared reading: *Galileo and the Starry Messenger* pp. 4–6	(close reading:) *Galileo and the Starry Messenger* pp. 7–9	constellation activity	(close reading:) *Galileo and the Starry Messenger* pp. 10–15	build your own telescope activity
Social Studies	finish final project on the Dark Ages	groups present final projects on the Dark Ages	(close reading:) *The Italian Renaissance* (textbook chapter intro)	lecture and class discussion of Renaissance changes	Renaissance art
Mathematics	review: graphing	assessment: graphing	small-group work: graphing and measurement review	lecture: finding volume	(close reading:) *Count Like an Egyptian: A Hands-On Introduction to Ancient Mathematics* pp. 1–2
Other	practice for spring assembly performance	(close reading:) visual literacy lesson on Van Gogh's *The Starry Night*	practice for spring assembly performance	little buddy time with kindergarten partners	begin Renaissance stained glass art project

Organization of this Book

We have created this resource with some very specific goals in mind. First, we want to support teachers in implementing close reading in ways that demonstrate intentional, explicit instruction. In other words, we want to take the guesswork out of the process and provide a research-supported approach that can easily fit into classroom lessons. Second, we want to provide instructional examples of close reading that demonstrate how it can be used to address other important classroom goals, such as general reading and writing goals, the development of academic language, inquiry learning, use of technology, deep thinking, and reading across disciplines.

Finally, it is important to us that we provide a close reading toolkit that includes sample texts, sample student activities, sample performance tasks, and other supports teachers can use to create close reading lessons. A close reading resource is only truly useful if it includes the tools needed to incorporate the approach into every area of the curriculum. For this reason, we have decided to present the majority of this book in a format that supports teachers' efforts to create close reading lessons for classroom use.

Digital Download

The planning templates, appendix resources, and sample lesson passages included in this book are available as Adobe® PDFs online. A complete list of the available documents is on pages 267–269. Additionally, the filenames are referenced throughout the book. To access the digital resources, go to http://www.tcmpub.com/download-files and enter the following code: 44168034. Follow the on-screen directions.

Guide to Book Sections

Section One is an overview of the close reading approach. In previous sections, the structure of close reading, useful terms, and frequently asked questions were reviewed.

Section Two presents the process for planning a close reading lesson. This is the section you should turn to as you are thinking about how to make initial planning decisions for a close reading session. Close reading requires careful preparation on the part of the teacher. There are several crucial decisions to be made. First, it is necessary to select an appropriate text. You will also decide which standard or standards to address and identify the areas of complexity for your students. Lastly, you will plan text-dependent questions and additional scaffolded questions. It is important to note that the text-dependent questions can, and should, evolve during the course of the lesson. You may anticipate that students will struggle with the main idea (and therefore need additional scaffold questions), but upon viewing their first-read annotations, realize that they instead struggled with a challenging vocabulary term. In that case, you might modify your initial text-dependent questions to include questions that lead students

Digital Download

A digital download with planning templates, appendix resources, and sample lesson passages accompanies this book.

to scrutinize the surrounding context or parts of the word to clarify the challenging term. Section Two will walk you through each of these steps explicitly.

Section Three presents the process for teaching a close reading lesson. This section includes detailed descriptions of how to scaffold the lesson for students of all reading levels. Throughout a close reading lesson, there are several more decisions that need to be made to determine how to scaffold the instruction for students. *Who will be doing the reading? How many times should students revisit the text? How will the lesson be chunked? What annotations should be used? What types of student resources are needed?*

Section Four presents simple step-by-step techniques for assessing and extending close reading lessons. This section includes specific guidelines, activities, templates for anecdotal records and performance tasks, and suggestions on how to reteach information to students who have not fully grasped a lesson. The final set of decisions for a close reading lesson surround the specific ways to assess students' understanding. You should create and use both formative and summative assessments to determine what, if anything, must be retaught.

Section Five and **Section Six** present a collection of close reading lessons. For each grade level, there are three literary and three informational texts with corresponding lessons. These lessons address a range of college and career readiness anchor standards, specifically key ideas and details, craft and structure, and integration of knowledge and ideas.

Finally, the **Appendices** are designed to help you scaffold lessons for a diverse group of students. Appendix B is a glossary of reteaching ideas, and Appendix C lists the graphic organizers and templates that are provided in the **Digital Download**. For example, there is a character web graphic organizer and a plot chart to be used for teaching text structure. There is also a T-chart and a guide for identifying figurative language to assist with vocabulary development.

The sections of this book are organized around the decisions to be made at each stage of planning and teaching a close reading lesson. Table 1.3 provides an overview of the decisions made at each stage.

Table 1.3 Close Reading Stages and Decisions

Close Reading Stage	What Decision Must Be Made?
Preplanning	• Identify a standard and lesson purpose. • Select a text. • Determine the areas of complexity. • Create text-dependent questions.
Teaching	• Determine how to scaffold the close read. • Who is doing the close reading? • How many times do students revisit the text? • Does any minor frontloading need to occur after the first reading? • How should the text be chunked? • What types of annotations should be used? • What types of student resources are needed?
Assessing and Extending	• How do I assess student understanding? • How do I assess student understanding during the lesson? • How do I assess student understanding after the lesson? • What do I do for students who, at the end of close reading, have not fully comprehended the text? • What do I do to reteach the students who did not understand? • How do I extend learning for those who successfully analyzed the text? • What extension tasks are appropriate for all of the students?

Try It!

Using Table 1.2 (page 14) as a model, describe potential places in which you can incorporate close reading into your instructional schedule. Write on the table below, or use the digital copy of the table from the Digital Download (incorporatingclosereading.pdf).

Incorporating Close Reading

Content Area	Monday	Tuesday	Wednesday	Thursday	Friday
Language Arts					
Science					
Social Studies					
Mathematics					
Other					

Section 2:
Planning Close Reading

Close reading is a unique instructional approach because it cannot be totally preplanned. The teacher designs the overall outline of the lesson, and the carefully selected text influences much of the learning. However, with each dive into the text, the discussion and learning follow students' needs. During a successful close reading lesson, you should be both prepared and flexible. Table 2.1 lists the areas of planning and decision making. The shaded areas will be addressed in Section Four of this book.

Table 2.1: Planning for Close Reading

Planning	Date: _____ Grade: _____ Discipline: _____ Purpose(s): _____ Standard(s):_____ Text Selection (literary or informational):_____ Performance Assessment: _____ Materials: _____
Text Selection	Title: _____ Author: _____ Page(s) or Section(s): _____ How should this text be chunked? _____ _____
Areas of Complexity	Lexile Level:_____ Meaning or Purpose:_____ Structure: _____ Language Features:_____ Knowledge Demands: _____
Text-Dependent Questions	1. _____ 2. _____ 3. _____ 4. _____ 5. _____
Performance Task	_____ _____ _____ _____

Differentiation

Additional Support: _____

Extension: _____

Identifying a Standard and Lesson Purpose

The first step in any lesson is to decide what to teach and why. Begin by considering the standards that will be addressed, the skills on which to focus, and the knowledge of language students already possess. We have selected and built our sample lessons around the applicable standards from the Common Core State Standards for English/Language Arts (2010) to meet the expectations of college and career readiness. Many state standards parallel these expectations. If the standard chosen is particularly challenging, you may opt to focus the lesson entirely around that one. However, often it is useful to bundle several standards into one lesson. Table 2.2 lists the five steps to take in preparing your lesson purpose(s) based on the standards chosen.

Steps for Identifying a Standard and Creating a Lesson Purpose

1. Choose a standard from the college and career readiness standards or state standards.

2. Create a lesson purpose in kid-friendly language.

3. Share the lesson purpose with your students.

4. Post the lesson purpose where all students can easily view it.

5. Translate the lesson purpose into an "I Can" statement that helps students self-assess.

Once you have selected your standards, they should be translated into a lesson purpose to be shared with your students. The purpose statements, also known as learning goals or intentions, should be thought of in two ways: *what* students are learning and *how* they are learning it. The goal of writing purpose statements is to make explicit, for students and teachers, what learning is occurring and how they can demonstrate that learning. Avoid writing purpose statements that are solely task or activity oriented. This might lead students to mistakenly think that learning is achieved through writing lists, completing graphic organizers, or presenting orally. Instead, purpose statements that describe the actual content to be learned teach students that by writing lists, completing graphic organizers, or presenting orally, they can demonstrate their understanding of the content.

All lesson tasks will be tied to the lesson purpose, so it is important that it clearly articulates what the teacher is teaching and is general enough to encompass the learning goal. For example, imagine that your class is reading a text about insects. You have identified several pertinent standards including identifying the main topic and retelling the details of a text. You can articulate to students *what* they will learn by writing the purpose statement: "You will identify the parts of an insect." Additionally, you can share with students *how* they will demonstrate their learning with the purpose statement: "You will create a drawing of an insect that shows its parts."

Examples of Student-Friendly Purpose Statements and "I Can" Statements

- **WHAT**: You will learn the five senses.

  HOW: Point to the parts of your body used for each of the five senses.

  I CAN: I can point to the parts of my body used for each of my senses.

- **WHAT**: Understand a character.

  HOW: Describe how Amazing Grace feels at the beginning, middle, and end o the story.

  I CAN: I can describe a character's feelings.

- **WHAT**: Understand where animals live.

  HOW: Glue pictures of animals to pictures of their correct homes.

  I CAN: I can show and describe where different animals live.

- **WHAT**: Examine emotion words.

  HOW: Draw faces and label the emotion of each.

  I CAN: I can describe emotion words.

- **WHAT**: Remember the order of events in a story.

  HOW: Put story pictures in order.

  I CAN: I can put story events in order.

Lastly, the purpose statements can be translated into "I Can" statements. These are student-generated sentences that students use to state what they are able to do. For example, if the purpose of the lesson is for students to understand the features of the planet Mars, and if the students will demonstrate their learning by listing five key details in a summary paragraph, the "I Can" statement might be, "I can list key details about the features of the planet Mars." At the end of the lessons, students assess themselves and decide if they can truthfully make this statement.

By sharing the purpose statements with your students, you provide them with contexts and goals around which to structure their own reading. It encourages them to stay focused. Post the purposes in the front of the classroom so that both you and the students can reference them often and have visual reminders of the current learning goals and how to achieve them.

Selecting a Text

The next step is to select the text. In many cases, you may wish to plan a close reading lesson focusing on a short, complex subsection of a larger text already being studied. Or you may wish to select a text specifically to engage in a close reading experience. In either case, it is important to evaluate the selected text for appropriate complexity and length. The close reading approach can be used for any lesson that involves a short passage that is of sufficient complexity to offer a challenge for your students. Additionally, it can also be used to closely examine charts, graphs, graphics, cartoons, or other visual elements. However, we will focus on print texts for our examples. Feel free to extrapolate the method to work with other kinds of reading material. If a text does not seem easily accessible to your students, then it may be complex enough to engage students in a close reading.

Research has shown that in order to be effective, texts selected for close reading should be "compact, short, self-contained ones that can be read and reread deliberately and slowly" (Coleman and Pimentel 2012, 4).

You might notice that it is repeatedly mentioned that the close reading approach is best for short texts. This is because it is an intensive and deep reading approach. The goal is that students will use the skills gained during the close reading experiences in your classroom whenever they are faced with a challenging text of any length, either in school or on their own. However, to tackle a larger text in a classroom setting can become unwieldy and daunting.

That is definitely not the goal! The classroom use of close reading should provide students with opportunities to develop and practice skills that will be useful to them for a lifetime. Thus, when choosing texts, keep in mind the time requirements, and make sure to not overwhelm yourself or your students.

There are several questions to keep in mind when selecting a text:

- Does it relate to the identified standards?

- Is it a text that is worthy of deep study and critical analysis?

- Is it relevant, interesting, and engaging?

- Does it fall within the range of the students' abilities, plus a little more? Will it make students stretch to gain full understanding?

- What are the demands of the text? (e.g., language, structure, knowledge)

- What scaffolds may be needed when tackling this text with the class? (e.g., *Will some students benefit from small-group instruction? Is it necessary to partner this text with another, less complex text to build background knowledge and language as scaffolding for struggling students?*)

Determining Areas of Complexity

When evaluating text complexity for students, there are three aspects to consider: the quantitative text attributes, the qualitative text attributes, and the reader/task attributes.

Quantitative Text Attributes

Quantitative text attributes are those that can be measured using numeric evaluations. These include sentence length, number of syllables, word length, and word frequency. The quantitative attributes of a text can be calculated using computer programs and reported with numeric designations. In the past, they were generally reported with grade-level designations, such as 4.6 (fourth grade, sixth month). However, there are several analysis systems that have come to favor and provide more information than simple grade-level designations, such as the Lexile® Framework for Reading.

The Lexile text measurement evaluates one dimension of text complexity and represents the quantitative attributes of text with a numeric designation. There is no absolute mapping of the Lexile scores with specific grade levels; instead, students are expected to read within a Lexile range or "Lexile band." For example, students in second grade should be comfortably reading within the 450L–730L band. Those same students should be challenged to read within the 420L–820L "Stretch" Lexile band. See Table 2.2 for a complete Lexile band chart.

Table 2.2 Lexile Band Chart

Grade Band	Current Lexile Band	"Stretch" Lexile Band*
K–1	N/A	N/A
2–3	450L–730L	420L–820L
4–5	640L–850L	740L–1010L
6–8	860L–1010L	925L–1185L
9–10	960L–1120L	1050L–1335L
11–CCR	1070L–1220L	1185L–1385L

*Common Core State Standards for English, Language Arts, Appendix A (Additional Information), NGA and CCSSO 2012

Other common leveling systems include DRA Levels, and Fountas & Pinnell's F&P Text Level Gradient™. Each of these systems attempts to provide graduated, quantitative assessment of text difficulty. Table 2.3 (page 24) shows the levels common to each grade.

Table 2.3 Other Leveling Systems

Grade Level	DRA Level	Fountas & Pinnell
Kindergarten	A–4	A–D
1	6–18	E–J
2	20–28	K–M
3	30–38	N–P
4	40	Q–S
5	50	T–V
6	60	W–Y

Leveling systems are good tools for evaluating the quantitative attributes of texts, but they cannot reflect the content of the text. For example, what if a text requires understanding of historic context to illuminate its subject? What if there is symbolism, a weighty central theme, or a challenging social dynamic at play? These attributes cannot be reflected in a quantitative metric. Therefore, it is essential to go beyond the quantitative elements when evaluating text complexity for students and delve into qualitative text attributes.

Qualitative Text Attributes

Qualitative text attributes are those text attributes that cannot be easily measured using a numeric value. These include text structures, author's purpose, language features, and the meaning of the text. The level of challenge included in these attributes of the text must be carefully analyzed and evaluated before the text is chosen for a group of students. Just because a text uses simple words does not necessarily mean that the text is not complex. Certain authors are known for choosing accessible language to convey nuanced topics. For example, pick any book by Ernest Hemingway or John Steinbeck, and you may discover that simply by looking at its quantitative attributes, it is simple enough to be read by most elementary students. In fact, Hemingway's *The Sun Also Rises* has a Lexile level of 610, which means that it should be easily decoded by an average third grader. But when qualitative attributes such as author's purpose and meaning are considered, the text is revealed to be much more complex.

Another important consideration included in qualitative text attributes is the *knowledge demand,* or amount of background knowledge a reader must have to discern the full meaning. For example, in reading a text about the Underground Railroad, a student must have a relatively deep knowledge of cultural concepts before beginning: *What is slavery? What is a railroad? Who were the abolitionists? What were the dangers for escaped slaves and those who helped them? What prevented escaped slaves from traveling through normal modes of conveyance?* Even if the text gives a lot of support and context, a reader lacking at least some familiarity with the time period and issues involved may find seemingly simple text deceptively challenging.

Authors write with audiences in mind. As we write this text, we envision it being read by professional educators who are engaging students in close reading practices. As we write, we tailor the information and tone to our audience—you. If you are not a member of our expected audience group, this book may be extremely challenging, indeed! We have not included a detailed summary of modern educational practices to place the close reading approach in context. If we did, our actual target audience would become impatient and bored. Authors of every genre must balance the knowledge demands of their writing.

If the author provides less support, the reader must put in more effort to attain a proper understanding. This struggle can be very healthy and rewarding and should not be universally avoided. But if the struggle becomes unproductive or frustrating, it can become difficult for a reader to stay motivated to stick with the reading. Unfortunately, there is no numerical value one can assign to the knowledge demands of a text. To adequately analyze text complexity, it is imperative to consider the specific students who will be reading it.

The next qualitative aspect to consider when evaluating a text is its structure and organization. For narrative texts, consider whether the piece is written using a linear plotline, or if it utilizes flashbacks, flash forwards, or other non-linear storytelling techniques. For elementary students, a straightforward, linear approach is usually easier to navigate. When evaluating informational texts, look closely at how the information is presented. Informational texts can utilize a number of structures, such as cause/effect, sequence, compare/contrast, and problem/solution. A text that sticks to one approach is typically less complex than one that includes a few. For example, consider a book that sequentially describes the process of a seed growing into a tree. All other things being equal, that book will be less complex than a text that starts out sequentially describing the seed growth process, jumps to cause and effect of the rainy season on seed growth, compares and contrasts the growth rates of a variety of seeds, and then tackles the problems and solutions of human encroachment on rainforest biomes.

Visual layout and visual support features play another part in determining the complexity of a text in terms of structure. There is sometimes a tendency to discount these features as outside the realm of "reading," but every aspect of a document factors into its complexity. Clarifying charts, maps, illustrations, and diagrams serve to simplify or extend the information already presented in the narrative. Likewise, font and layout choices affect the reader's comprehension. Clear, simple, uncluttered visual features tend to make even complex texts accessible. Busy fonts, multiple-column layouts, and ambiguously placed visual support features actually obscure the meaning of the text and make reading more challenging. Even a particularly sophisticated or hyper-informative map or chart can complicate an otherwise simple text.

The way the author handles relationships among ideas is an important component of the text organization that affects text complexity. Consider relationships between characters, plots, and subplots in narrative texts. For informational texts, relationships exist between main ideas, facts and details, or abstract and concrete concepts. When these relationships are simpler, the text is likely to be simpler. When the relationships increase in complexity, so does the text.

Another major area to consider when evaluating qualitative text attributes is how various language features affect the complexity of the text. As a general rule, a more conversational writing style will make a text more accessible and less complex. More formally written textbooks, while an essential part of a student's education, often increase complexity with their less familiar language style. Likewise, the use of metaphors, similes, descriptive language, onomatopoeia, personification, and other literary devices, this can make a narrative text's meaning more obscure and less comprehensible.

Vocabulary plays multiple roles in the complexity of a text. Words can be easily evaluated quantitatively based on length, number of syllables, and frequency of use in the English language. However, there are cultural aspects of vocabulary that clearly require qualitative evaluation. *Are these words commonly and currently used in this geographical area and in this way?* should be a question that goes through one's mind. Archaic, author-created, or culturally unfamiliar vocabulary can significantly increase the complexity of a text, providing layers of meaning and interest, while forcing the reader to return repeatedly in search of context clues. Dr. Seuss books are well known for their creative use of language, and, in fact, their creation of language. For example, consider this excerpt from *The Lorax*.

The Lorax
by Dr. Seuss

"Sir! You are crazy with greed.

There is no one on earth

Who would buy that fool Thneed!"

But the very next minute, I proved he was wrong.

For just at that minute, a chap came along,

and he thought that the Thneed I had knitted was great.

He happily bought it for three ninety-eight.

As is evident, the use of author-created words, such as *Thneed*, as well as the archaic/British term *chap* can increase the text complexity in ways that quantitative analysis might miss. However, these linguistic oddities also create layers of interest and depth in the passage. The various ways that authors choose to present and play with language creates a more meaningful and enjoyable experience for readers, but they also serve to add complexity to the text.

The meaning of the text and the author's purpose in writing it are two other important qualitative attributes to consider. The meaning of the text refers to the sophistication of the ideas and how overtly they are laid out in the writing. For example, *Watership Down*, by Richard Adams, is, on its surface, the adventures of a group of rabbits. However, when one takes into account its allegorical themes, one realizes that the story is much more nuanced, deeper, and more meaningful than a superficial assessment might expose. Despite the rabbit on the cover, this text is appropriate for a secondary classroom. Before using a book in a classroom, you need to fully evaluate the layers of meaning for your text choice.

Like meaning, an author's purpose may be clearly stated, implied, or even intentionally hidden. When evaluating how the author's purpose affects the complexity of a text, one of the most important factors to consider is how, or if, this purpose is expressed. This can be particularly critical in informational texts where the author may be overtly or slyly trying to influence the reader's opinions on a topic. It is important to remember that every author has a perspective, and sometimes these can be particularly important when building an understanding of a text. When the author's purpose is subtle, uncovering it may be challenging, and thus, the text may prove to be more complex than one in which the author divulges up front his or her reason for writing the text. See Table 2.4 for an example of one teacher's evaluation of the first page of E. B. White's *Charlotte's Web* for a close reading lesson.

Table 2.4 Sample Qualitative Evaluation: *Charlotte's Web*

Qualitative Measures	Degree of Difficulty	Explanation
Meaning or Purpose	Medium	The passage explicitly states the main ideas, but certain details require inference to fully understand. While the basic theme is friendship, death and natural life cycles are also prominent.
Structure	Medium	The structure of the passage is conventional and chronological but utilizes dialogue and different character voices, which make comprehension more difficult.
Language Features	High	The language is descriptive, sometimes idiomatic, and a bit archaic. The text assumes familiarity with some terminology associated with farming and rural life.
Knowledge Demands	Med–High	The text assumes cultural knowledge about farming life. The death of animals is presented directly with no preface. Students who have not considered where the meat they eat comes from might be jarred by the very first page.

Tables 2.5 and 2.6 (pages 29–36) provide scoring rubrics that help in evaluating the qualitative attributes of literary and informational texts.

Table 2.5 Qualitative Attributes Scoring Rubric for Literary Texts

Qualitative Rubric for Literary Texts

What Does the Text Say?

Dimension	Consideration	Scoring = 1 Easy or Comfortable Text	Scoring = 2 Moderate or Grade-Level Text	Scoring = 3 Challenging or Stretch Text
Meaning or Purpose	Meaning	The text contains simple ideas with one level of meaning conveyed through obvious literary devices.	The text contains some complex ideas with more than one level of meaning conveyed through subtle literary devices.	The text includes substantial ideas with several levels of inferred meaning conveyed through highly sophisticated literary devices.
	Main Ideas and Key Details	Main ideas and key details support the story theme and character development.	Main ideas and key details weakly support the story theme and character development.	Main ideas and key details that support the story theme or character development are not apparent; much is left to the interpretation of the reader.

Qualitative Rubric for Literary Texts (cont.)

How Does the Text Work?

Dimension	Consideration	Scoring = 1 Easy or Comfortable Text	Scoring = 2 Moderate or Grade-Level Text	Scoring = 3 Challenging or Stretch Text
Structure	Organization	The text follows a simple, conventional chronological plot pattern with few or no shifts in point of view or time; plot is highly predictable.	The text organization is somewhat unconventional; may have two or more storylines and some shifts in time and point of view; plot is sometimes hard to predict.	The text organization is intricate and unconventional with multiple subplots and shifts in time and point of view; plot is unpredictable.
	Visual Supports and Layout	Text placement is consistent throughout the text and includes a large, readable font. Illustrations directly support text content.	Text placement may include columns, text interrupted by illustrations, or other variations; uses a smaller font size. Illustrations support the text directly but may include images that require synthesis of text.	Text placement includes columns and many inconsistencies as well as very small font size. Few illustrations support the text directly; most require deep analysis and synthesis.
	Relationships Among Ideas	Relationships among ideas or characters are clear and obvious.	Relationships among ideas or characters are subtle and complex.	Relationships among ideas or characters are complex, embedded, and must be inferred.
	Vocabulary	Vocabulary is accessible, familiar, and can be determined through context clues.	Vocabulary combines familiar terms with academic vocabulary appropriate to the grade level.	Vocabulary includes extensive academic vocabulary, including many unfamiliar terms.

Qualitative Rubric for Literary Texts *(cont.)*

What Does the Text Mean?

Dimension	Consideration	Scoring = 1 Easy or Comfortable Text	Scoring = 2 Moderate or Grade-Level Text	Scoring = 3 Challenging or Stretch Text
Structure *(cont.)*	Author's Style and Tone	The style of the text is explicit and easy to comprehend, and the tone is conversational.	The style of the text combines explicit and complex meanings, and the tone is somewhat formal.	The style of the text is abstract, and the language is ambiguous and generally unfamiliar. The tone may be somewhat unfamiliar to readers, such as an ironic tone.
	Author's Purpose	The purpose of the text is simple, clear, concrete, and easy to identify.	The purpose of the text is somewhat subtle, requires interpretation, or is abstract.	The purpose of the text is abstract, implicit, may be ambiguous, and is revealed through the totality of the text.
	Theme	The author explicitly states the theme or message of the text.	The theme or message of the text may not be stated directly, but can be inferred by the reader.	The theme or message of the text is not stated directly by the author and must be inferred through careful reading of the text.
	Point of View	The story is told from a single point of view (first, second, or third person) throughout.	The story is told from more than one point of view and may incorporate multiple characters' points of view that are identified by the reader.	The story is told from multiple points of view, including the viewpoints of different characters, and is not always easily identified by the reader.

Qualitative Rubric for Literary Texts *(cont.)*

What Does the Text Mean? *(cont.)*

Dimension	Consideration	Scoring = 1 Easy or Comfortable Text	Scoring = 2 Moderate or Grade-Level Text	Scoring = 3 Challenging or Stretch Text
Language Features	Use of Language	The author uses a limited amount of symbolism or figurative language; language is explicit and can be literally interpreted.	The author conveys the meaning through some use of figurative language, including imagery, metaphor, symbolism, simile, and personification, but also includes examples and explanations that support interpreting the meaning.	The author conveys the meaning through extensive use of figurative language and provides very limited explanation.
	Standard English	The text is written using a language register and/or form that is familiar to the reader (as opposed to an unfamiliar form like Old English or extensive uses of dialect).	The text is written using a language register and/or form that contains some language conventions and vernacular that are not familiar to the reader.	The text is written using a language register and/or form that includes extensive variations of standard English that are uncommon to the reader.
Knowledge Demands	Background Knowledge	Experiences portrayed are common life experiences; everyday cultural or literary knowledge is required.	Experiences portrayed include both common and less common experiences; some cultural, historical, or literary background knowledge is required.	Experiences portrayed are unfamiliar to most readers. The text requires extensive depth of topical, historical, or literary background knowledge.
	Cultural Knowledge	Content addresses common cultural and historical knowledge that is familiar.	Content addresses some cultural knowledge that may not be familiar.	Content includes heavy references to cultural or historical knowledge that is not readily familiar to those from other cultures.

Table 2.6 Qualitative Attributes Scoring Rubric for Informational Texts

Qualitative Rubric for Informational Texts

What Does the Text Say?

Dimension	Consideration	Scoring = 1 Easy or Comfortable Text	Scoring = 2 Moderate or Grade-Level Text	Scoring = 3 Challenging or Stretch Text
Meaning or Purpose	Meaning	The information is clear, and concepts are concretely explained.	The information includes complex, abstract ideas and extensive details.	The information is abstract, intricate, and may be highly theoretical.
	Main Ideas and Key Details	Key ideas and details that support the central theme are explicitly stated.	Some key ideas and details are explicitly stated, but others must be inferred.	Key ideas and details that would support comprehension must be inferred.

Qualitative Rubric for Informational Texts *(cont.)*

How Does the Text Work?

Dimension	Consideration	Scoring = 1 Easy or Comfortable Text	Scoring = 2 Moderate or Grade-Level Text	Scoring = 3 Challenging or Stretch Text
Structure	Organization	The text adheres primarily to a single expository text structure and focuses on facts.	The text employs multiple expository text structures, includes facts and/or a thesis, and demonstrates characteristics common to a particular discipline.	The text organization is intricate, may combine multiple structures or genres, is highly abstract, includes multiple theses, and demonstrates sophisticated organization appropriate to a particular discipline.
	Visual Supports and Layout	Text placement is consistent throughout and includes a large, readable font. Text features like simple charts, graphs, photos, tables, diagrams, and headings directly support the text and are easy to understand.	Text placement may include columns, text interrupted by illustrations or other variations, and a smaller font size. Text features like complex charts, graphs, photos, tables, diagrams, headings, and subheadings support the text but require interpretation.	Text placement includes columns and many inconsistencies as well as very small font size. Text features like intricate charts, graphs, photos, tables, diagrams, headings, and subheadings are not supported by the text and require inference and synthesis of information.
	Relationships Among Ideas	Relationships among concepts, processes, or events are clear and explicitly stated.	Relationships among some concepts, processes, or events may be implicit and subtle.	Relationships among concepts, processes, and events are intricate, deep, and subtle.
	Vocabulary	Some vocabulary is subject-specific, but the text includes many terms familiar to students that are supported by context clues.	The vocabulary is subject-specific, includes many unfamiliar terms, and provides limited support through context clues.	Vocabulary is highly academic, subject-specific, demanding, nuanced, and very context dependent.

Qualitative Rubric for Informational Texts *(cont.)*

What Does the Text Mean?

Dimension	Consideration	Scoring = 1 Easy or Comfortable Text	Scoring = 2 Moderate or Grade-Level Text	Scoring = 3 Challenging or Stretch Text
Meaning or Purpose (Vocabulary, and Craft, Style) *(cont.)*	Author's Style and Tone	The style is simple and conversational and conveys a casual tone. It may incorporate narrative elements with simple sentences containing a few concepts.	The style is objective, featuring passive constructions, highly factual content, some nominalization, and compound or complex sentences. The tone is generally formal, but may have some conversational aspects.	The style is specialized to a discipline, contains dense concepts and high nominalization, and features compound and complex sentences. The tone is distant, extremely formal and written in third person.
	Author's Purpose	The purpose of the text is simple, clear, concrete, and easy to identify.	The purpose of the text is somewhat subtle or abstract and requires interpretation.	The purpose of the text is very subtle or abstract and requires extensive interpretation.
	Theme	The author states the theme or message of the text explicitly.	The theme or message of the text may not be stated directly, but can be easily inferred by the reader.	The theme or message of the text is not stated directly by the author and must be inferred through careful reading of the text.
	Point of View	The author's perspective or point of view about a topic or issue is clearly stated within the text.	The author's perspective or point of view about a topic or issue may not be stated directly, but can be easily inferred by the reader.	The author's perspective or point of view about a topic or issue is not directly stated and must be inferred by the reader through careful analysis of the text.

Qualitative Rubric for Informational Texts *(cont.)*

What Does the Text Mean? *(cont.)*

Dimension	Consideration	Scoring = 1 Easy or Comfortable Text	Scoring = 2 Moderate or Grade-Level Text	Scoring = 3 Challenging or Stretch Text
Language Features	Use of Language	The author uses common, discipline-related language that is explicit and can be literally interpreted.	The author uses language that is related to the discipline but less familiar to someone new to the discipline. Examples and explanations that support interpreting the meaning are included.	The author conveys the meaning through extensive use of highly sophisticated, discipline-based language and does not include supports for interpretation.
	Standard English	The text is written using a language register and/or form that is familiar to the reader.	The language used contains some language conventions and vernacular that are not familiar to the reader.	The language used includes extensive variations of standard English that are unfamiliar to the reader.
Knowledge Demands	Background Knowledge	The content addresses common information familiar to students.	The content addresses somewhat technical information that requires some background knowledge to understand fully.	The content is highly technical and contains specific information that requires deep background knowledge to understand fully.
	Cultural Knowledge	Content addresses common cultural and historical knowledge that is familiar.	Content addresses some cultural knowledge that may not be familiar.	Content includes heavy references to cultural or historical knowledge that is not readily familiar to those from other cultures.

Reader/Task Attributes

A final element of text complexity to evaluate when looking at a potential classroom text isn't about the text itself. It is about the students in the classroom and their own readiness for approaching the chosen text and its associated learning and performance tasks. The reader/task attributes describe elements of text complexity that are specific to a reader (i.e., reading experience, background knowledge, and motivation) and specific to the tasks for which the text will be used (i.e., recording basic facts, enjoying a narrative, or deeply understanding nuance). If the reading task is to identify and sequence the events leading to the American Revolution, the reader may be successful using a wide range of texts. However, a more nuanced task, like comprehending multiple perspectives and motivations leading to the American Revolution, would require a more careful match of reader and text. Likewise, a history buff who has acquired a lot of background knowledge on the American Revolution is likely to successfully comprehend an American Revolution text that seems to be just out of his or her reach according to quantitative measures.

Close reading lessons and the role of the teacher during those lessons will be significantly different depending on the topical readiness and knowledge of close reading of the students. If the students have a strong background in close reading, obviously the teacher will need to do less modeling and will be able to tackle more complicated tasks throughout the lesson. On the other hand, if students are unaccustomed to the demands of close reading—perhaps they are used to skimming for content, skipping over unknown words, moving forward without fully understanding the content of what they have read—then it will be important to slow down the process and guide students to develop the necessary skills.

There are four areas to evaluate when considering the readiness of students for the close reading of complex texts: reading and cognitive skills, prior knowledge and experience, motivation and engagement, and specific task concerns. Let us consider each of these areas with the following short poem.

Bed in Summer
by Robert Louis Stevenson

In winter I get up at night
And dress by yellow candle-light.
In summer, quite the other way,
I have to go to bed by day.
I have to go to bed and see
The birds still hopping on the tree,
Or hear the grown-up people's feet
Still going past me in the street.
And does it not seem hard to you,
When all the sky is clear and blue,
And I should like so much to play,
To have to go to bed by day?

Reading and cognitive skills describe both the literal comprehension skills and the deeper-level thinking skills needed to approach the chosen text and dig deeply into it. Think about the level of decoding that students display. Consider their ability to focus on the details and make inferences. Different students and different classes will require varying amounts of scaffolding to achieve full comprehension of a challenging text. In "Bed in Summer," students may understand that the child in the poem is frustrated by having to go to bed while the sun is out. However, they may need scaffolding to fully gather that the sun comes up later in the winter and stays out longer in the summer.

Prior knowledge and experience include what students have lived and studied. Have students had experiences with close reading before? Are they familiar with the type of writing, topic, and style of the text chosen? In "Bed in Summer," students will probably be familiar with this rhyming couplet form of poetry from nursery rhymes. Also, the subject of longer days during summer and shorter days during winter may be something they have experienced. However, if students grew up near the equator, or are from a sub-culture that does not require children to sleep before sundown during the summer, there may be experience gaps to bridge while delving into this poem.

The area of motivation and engagement addresses affective needs. Sometimes, students can be put off by the format of a text or the subject matter. "Bed in Summer" is both short and accessible, but it will be necessary to closely consider your students' reactions to poetry in order to determine if they need reassurance and assistance in engaging with a poetic text. Subject matter can also draw students in or push them away. Knowing topics of interest can increase student motivation and engagement, as they allow students to enjoy the process of close reading any type of text.

Specific task concerns include the impact of the tasks students are being asked to complete. Even if students are ready for a particular piece of text, it is important not to underestimate the challenge of the associated tasks. Let us suppose the task in this example is to describe the perspective of the narrator using prose. It is unlikely that every student in the class will be able to accomplish this task without some scaffolding. However, if you provide a graphic organizer for students to record specific ideas and details from the poem, the task becomes more manageable for all students.

Creating Text-Dependent Questions

Once you have determined the areas of complexity of a text, it is time to start thinking about the types of text-dependent questions to ask that help students hone in on the learning goals for the lesson. Your text-dependent questions will be based upon the areas of complexity you have identified. Text-dependent questions are great scaffolds for guiding students to use the text to uncover meaning. Text-dependent questions do not rely on a student's relationship to the topic, but instead tap into what the author embeds in the text itself. A simple way to identify a text-dependent question is that students cannot answer the question if they have not read the text or have the text read to them. Students cannot rely primarily on general life knowledge or personal connections to the topic to answer these types of questions.

Text-dependent questions are *not* all low-level inquiries designed to support literal recall. To the contrary, they can push students to dig incrementally deeper at each stage of reading. They require students to analyze and critically review the text and facilitate a deeper relationship with it as they repeatedly engage with it. So, how do teachers get started in creating them? They

→ begin by identifying key ideas in the text;

→ consider what questions might focus students on the gist of the text;

→ orient students toward key vocabulary and text structure used in the text (e.g., compare/contrast, problem/solution, cause/effect, or sequential);

→ craft questions that link to the purpose of the lesson;

→ determine and focus on the most challenging segment of the text based on the text complexity rubric; and

→ look at standards and derive questions that will focus students toward those goals.

To help get you started, we have provided some question stems in Table 2.7 (page 40). It may also be useful to peruse the questions embedded in the lessons. It is important to note in Section Five and Section Six that although you will create text-dependent questions as you plan each lesson, you will also revise, add, or delete any of the proposed questions that do not meet your students' needs as evidenced by your continuing assessment of their performance during the close reading. Furthermore, it is essential to frame questions for narrative texts differently from informational texts. For example, questions about plot, setting, and

Question Stems

When trying to lead students toward information embedded in a text, it is important not to begin with too much focus. It is better to start with the most general questions, then ask more and more pointed ones if they become necessary. Here are some examples:

EXAMPLE 1: What does the character mean? (general)

- What language does the character use? (more specific)

- What does the word _____ mean? (even more specific)

- How does using that word help us understand what the character means? (quite specific)

EXAMPLE 2: Why did the author write the information this way? (general)

- How does including the chart help us understand the main idea? (more specific)

- Look at the chart. Find information in the chart that helps support the main idea of the text. (even more specific)

- How do _____ (fact 1) and _____ (fact 2) from the chart help us understand that _____ (main idea of the text)? (quite specific) characters will likely not apply to informational texts. Think of the text-dependent questions as starting points. As you proceed, your lesson becomes a living and breathing experience, molded and shaped to meet students' needs. You will direct your questions to areas of the text students are struggling to clarify, giving them the most meaningful, purposeful experience possible and maximizing their learning.

Table 2.7 Common Question Stems for Text-Dependent Questions by Grade Level

Kindergarten Text-Dependent Questions	
Main Idea/ Theme	• What is the big idea of the text/story? Where do you find it? • How is _____ explained? Where does it say this in the text? • What is the big idea of paragraph/sentence _____? How can you tell?
Key Details	• What are the important details in this text/story? How do you know? • How does the author tell us about _____? • What is the big idea? What words tell you about it? • List three details from the text/story.
Summarizing	• Retell the story in your own words. • What happens in the text? • Tell the big events from the story in order.
Text Features	• Why does the author use the _____ (text feature)? What does it tell us? • What can we learn from _____ (text feature)? Why is it important to the text/story? • Look at the sidebar/graphic. What does it tell you? • Look at the headings. What do they help us know?
Text Structure	• Can this text/story really happen? How do you know? • Does this text tell a story or give information? How can you tell? • What words in the text do characters speak? How do you know? • What happens in the beginning? The middle? The end? • Who is telling the story? What would change if someone else told it?
Setting	• Where does this story happen? How can you tell? • How do the pictures help us understand the setting? • When does this story happen? How can you tell?

Kindergarten Text-Dependent Questions *(cont.)*

Plot	• What words tell about _____ (event)? • How do the pictures help us understand _____ (event)? • Why is _____ (event) important? • How does _____ (event) make _____ (character) feel/act? • What happens right before _____ (event)? What happens right after?
Characters/ Individuals	• What does _____ (character) look like? What words does the author use to help you make a picture in your head? • What does _____ (character) look like? How do the pictures help us understand this? • How does _____ (character/person) change during the story? • How does _____ (character/person) feel when _____ (event) happens? What words tell you? • What does _____ (character/person) want? How can you tell?
Point of View	• Who is telling the story? How do you know? • What is _____'s point of view? How can you tell? • How do _____ (character 1) and _____ (character 2) see things differently? How do you know? • How does the author feel about (subject/character)? How do you know?
Tone	• How does this story make you feel? Which words in the text make you feel that way?
Author's Purpose	• What is the author trying to tell us? • What question is the author trying to answer? • What does the author want us to understand? • Why did the author write this? How can you tell?
Language Usage	• Which words in the text/story show _____? How can you tell? • What are some other words that mean _____? Why do you think the author chose to use this word instead? • Reread paragraph/sentence #____. Without looking again, what words do you remember? Which words stand out? Why are they important?

Kindergarten Text-Dependent Questions *(cont.)*

Figurative Language	• Which words help you see/hear/smell _____? • How did the author "paint a picture" for you? Which words help? • Which words help you see _____ in your mind? • Why does the author have the _____ talk and act like a person?
Making Inferences	• Why does _____ (character) feel _____? What words in the text let you know? • What can you tell about _____? How do you know? • Reread sentence #_____. How does it help you guess what will happen next? • Think about the talk between _____ (character 1) and _____ (character 2). What do you think will happen next, based on what they say? • What does the author think about _____? How can you tell? • How do the pictures help us understand _____?

1st Grade Text-Dependent Questions

Main Idea/ Theme	• What is the main idea of the text/story? Where do you find it? • How is _____ explained? Use the text to tell how. • What is the main idea of paragraph/sentence _____? How can you tell?
Key Details	• What are the important details in this text/story? How do you know? • How does the author tell us about _____? • What is the main idea? What words in the text tell you more about it? • List one key detail from each paragraph/sentence. What do they tell us when you look at them all together?
Summarizing	• Retell the story in your own words. • What happens in the text? • What is the main event in the text? Tell the most important details about it. • Retell the main events of this text in order.
Text Features	• Why does the author use the _____ (text feature)? What does it tell us? • What information can we learn from _____ (text feature)? Why is this important to the text/story? • Look at the sidebar or graphic. What does it tell you? • Look at the headings. How do they help guide the reader? • Look at the table of contents/index. What kind of information does it show?
Text Structure	• Could this text really happen? How do you know? • Does this text tell a story or give information? How can you tell? • What words in the text do characters speak? How do you know? • What happens in the beginning? The middle? The end? • Who is telling the story? What would change if someone else told it? • Reread the start. Why does the author start the story that way?
Setting	• What is the setting? • Where does this story happen? Why does it matter? • When does this story happen? Why does it matter? • Tell what you know about the setting. Give details from the text.

1st Grade Text-Dependent Questions *(cont.)*

Plot	• What words tell about _____ (event)? Why does it happen? • Why is _____ (event) important? • How does _____ (event) affect _____ (character)? • What happens right before _____ (event)? What happens right after?
Characters/ Individuals	• What does _____ (character) look like? What words does the author use to help you get a picture in your head? • How does _____ (character) change during the story? • How does _____ (character) feel when _____ (event) happens? What words tell you? • What does _____ (character) want in the story? How can you tell?
Point of View	• Who is telling the story? How do you know? • What is _____'s point of view? How can you tell? • What is _____ (first character's) point of view? What is _____ (second character's) point of view? How are they different? • What does the author think about _____? How can you tell?
Tone	• How does this story make you feel? Which words/sentences help you to feel that way? • How does the author feel about (subject/character)? How do you know?
Author's Purpose	• What is the author trying to tell the reader? • What question is the author trying to answer in the text? • What does the author want the reader to understand? • Why did the author write this text? How can you tell?
Language Usage	• The word _____ can mean more than one thing. How can you tell which meaning it has here? • Which words in the text/story show _____? How can you tell? • What are some other words that mean _____? Why do you think the author chose to use this word instead? • Reread paragraph #_____. Without looking back at the text, what words do you remember? Which words stand out? Why are they important?

1st Grade Text-Dependent Questions *(cont.)*

Figurative Language	• Why does the author exaggerate? How does it help the story? • Which words help you see/hear/smell _____? • How did the author "paint a picture" for you? Which words help? • Which words help you see _____ in your mind? • Why does the author have the _____ talk and act like a person?
Making Inferences	• Why does _____ (character) feel _____? What words in the text let you know? • What can you tell about _____? How do you know? • Reread sentence #_____. How does it help you guess what will happen next? • Think about the talk between _____ (character 1) and _____ (character 2). Based on what they say, what do you think will happen next? • What does the author think about _____? How can you tell?

2nd Grade Text-Dependent Questions

Main Idea/ Theme	• Based on the events in the text, what is the main idea of the text? Find where it is stated in the text. • How does the _____ (paragraph/sentence) relate to the main idea? Use specific words and phrases from the text in your response. • How does the information in paragraphs/sentences # _____ and # _____ help you understand the main idea? • The main idea is not directly stated in the text. How do you know what it is? • What is the theme of the text? How do you know? • What is the moral of the text? How do you know?
Key Details	• What are the important details in this text/story? How do you know? • Why does the author put the supporting details in this order? Refer to the text to help you explain. • What details in _____ (paragraph/page) help to support the main idea? • List one key detail from each paragraph/sentence. What do they tell us when you look at them all together?

2nd Grade Text-Dependent Questions *(cont.)*

Summarizing	• Summarize the story in your own words. • Retell the story by listing the key details in order. • What is the main event in the text/story? Tell the most important details about it. • Retell the main events of this text/story in order. How is the order of events important?
Text Features	• Why does the author use the _____ (text feature)? What does it tell us? • What information can we learn from _____ (text feature)? Why is this important? • Look at the sidebar/graphic. What does it tell you? • Look at the headings. How do they help guide the reader? • Look at the table of contents/index. What kind of information does it show? How can you use it to find _____ in the book?
Text Structure	• Is this a true story? How do you know? • Does this text tell a story or give information? How can you tell? • Why does the author include conversation in the text? How does it help the text? • How does the way the author begins the text affect the middle? The end? Does this structure help your understanding or enjoyment of the text? Use the text to explain. • Who is narrating the text? How do you know? What would change if someone else told it? • Think of the order of events. Why does the author choose that order?
Setting	• Describe the setting. Use words from the text. • How does the setting influence the text? • When does this story happen? How would it change if it took place in a different time? • Tell what you know about the setting. Give details from the text.

2nd Grade Text-Dependent Questions *(cont.)*

Plot	• Why is _____ (event) important? Explain using words from the text. • How does _____ (event 1) relate to _____ (event 2)? • How does _____ (event) affect _____ (character)? • What happens right before _____ (event)? What happens right after? • What is the climax of the text? How can you tell?
Characters/ Individuals	• Describe _____ (character/person). What words does the author use to help you form a picture in your head? • How does _____ (character/person) change during the course of the text? • How does _____ (character/person) feel when _____ (event) happens? What words tell you? • What does the author want us to know about _____ (character/person)? How can you tell?
Point of View	• Who is telling the story? How do you know? • How does _____'s point of view differ from _____'s point of view? How can you tell? • How does the author show _____'s point of view over time? Does it change? Explain. • What is the author's point of view? How can you tell? • How does the author's/narrator's point of view influence how the text is told? • Does the author show more than one point of view in this text? How?
Tone	• How does this story make you feel? What words does the author use to help you feel that way? • Is the text positive or negative? Use details to show how you know. • How does the author feel about (subject/character)? How do you know? • Is the author an expert on _____? How can you tell?
Author's Purpose	• What is the author trying to tell the reader? • What question is the author trying to answer in the text? • Why does the author _____? • What does the author want the reader to understand? • Why did the author write this text? How can you tell?

2nd Grade Text-Dependent Questions *(cont.)*

Language Usage	• The word _____ can mean more than one thing. How can you tell which meaning it has here? • Which words in the text show _____? How can you tell? • What are some synonyms for _____? Why do you think the author chose to use this word instead? • Reread paragraph #_____. Without looking back at the text, what words do you remember? Which words stand out? Why are they important?
Figurative Language	• Why does the author use _____ (personification/metaphor/hyperbole/multiple-meaning words)? How does it help the text? • Which words help you see/hear/smell _____? • How does the author "paint a picture" in your mind? Which words help? • Which words help you see _____ in your mind?
Making Inferences	• Why does _____ (character) feel _____? What words in the text let you know? • What can you tell about _____? How do you know? • Reread sentence #_____. How does it help you predict what will happen next? • Think about the talk between _____ (character 1) and _____ (character 2). Predict what will happen next based on what they say. • What does the author think about _____? How can you tell? • What does the narrator think about _____? What words help you know?

Ordering Text-Dependent Questions

The final step to preplanning your lesson is to put the text-dependent questions into logical order. The questions should move students from general to specific and from lower-level analysis to higher-level analysis. The order should roughly mirror the skills described as one progresses through Anderson and Krathwohl's adaptation of Bloom's Taxonomy (2001). By the end, students should have a comprehensive relationship with the complexities of the text, be able to tackle the performance task, take an argumentative position concerning the stated learning goals, and craft an "I Can" statement that provides an assessment of their performance.

For example, begin your text-dependent questions by pinpointing the gist of the text, such as, "What is the text about?" and "What is the author trying to share?" These questions apply beginning-level thinking involving knowledge and comprehension. Then, move to questions that begin to press students for specifics. In this way, you move toward applying and analyzing the content of the text. For example, if the lesson revolves around explicit and implicit information, ask, "Which sentences give us explicit information about (the topic)?", or "Which sentences implicitly give us information about (the topic)?" Finally, transition into pushing students toward evaluating the deeper structure of the text and the synthesis of concepts woven throughout, such as, "Which sentences help us determine the theme of the text?", "What details help us more deeply understand this theme?", or "How does the author develop the theme over the course of the text?"

The text-dependent questions should ready students for the performance task assessment that concludes the close reading experience. We are not suggesting that the questions need to always be asked in this order. We are suggesting that you know what each question requires of students, and you ask questions that advance student learning. Begin with what they know. If they have a basic understanding of the topic, perhaps ask fewer questions about the specifics of what the text says and more questions about how the text works and what the text means.

Try It!

Directions: Analyze the passage below and plan for a close reading lesson. Use the guidelines and tables in this section along with your knowledge of your students to identify the areas of complexity and plan initial text-dependent questions. Write on the chart on the next page, or use the digital copy of the chart from the Digital Download (planningclosereading.pdf).

Be sure to tab or mark the pages you find most helpful to your work. These are the pages to which you can return when you plan actual lessons to use with your students.

Pretty in Pink (Lexile 570L)

Just when we think we've seen it all, along comes a giant pink surprise!

Park rangers in Australia have made a big discovery. They found large pink slugs that no one knew existed. But this slug species has been around for millions of years. It lives only on Mount Kaputar in Australia. Most of the time, the slugs stay hidden. But they come out after big rainstorms.

Australia was once covered in rainforests. But that was long ago. Much of Australia is dry now. Mount Kaputar is unique. Plants there are thick and colorful. Some living things that have died out everywhere else still live well there. The pink slug is one of those lucky animals.

The slug is about eight inches long. That makes it about twice the size of most other slugs. Its bright pink color helps it stay hidden among colorful leaves.

But the pink beauties are not the only new things the forest rangers found! They also spied three new species of snails. But these aren't just any snails. Oh, no! These snails are cannibals! They eat their own kind. These creepy creatures follow the trail left by other snails. And then, lunchtime!

Whether they are big and pink or creepy cannibals, no one will think of slugs and snails in the same way again!

Try It! *(cont.)*

Planning Chart for Close Reading

Planning

Date:_____ Grade: _____ Discipline:_____

Purpose(s): _____

Standard(s):_____

Text Selection (literary or informational):_____

Performance Assessment: _____

Materials: _____

Text Selection

Title:_____

Author: _____

Page(s) or Section(s): _____

How should this text be chunked? _____

_____

Areas of Complexity

Lexile Level:_____

Meaning or Purpose:_____

Structure: _____

Language Features:_____

Knowledge Demands: _____

Text-Dependent Questions

1. _____

2. _____

3. _____

4. _____

5. _____

Performance Task

_____

_____

_____

_____

Differentiation

Additional Support: _____

_____

Extension: _____

_____

Section 3:
Teaching Close Reading

Scaffolding in the Close Reading Approach

As you embark on a close reading experience with your class, it is important to consider how best to support close reading at the level specifically needed by your students to achieve the learning goals you have established. You know your class, so you must make individualized choices that will help to gradually remove scaffolding for all your students. Remember, the goal is for *every* student to be able to read and engage with the complex text that you have chosen. Student struggle is only useful inasmuch as it is productive. Proficiency will not be achieved by allowing student struggles to end in failure. Thus, carefully supporting your students throughout a close reading is essential. You must be ready to offer instructional scaffolds in the form of questions, prompts, and cues (such as reminding students of previously learned information or cueing them to look at a particular line of the text) throughout the experience. Constantly listen for issues that may arise, and assist students' progress throughout the process.

You have already identified the areas of challenge in your chosen text through the preplanning work of assessing the quantitative attributes and applying the appropriate qualitative rubric provided in Section Two. But there are some critical decisions that must be considered as you move forward.

- Who is doing the reading?
- How should the text be chunked?
- What sort of annotations should be used?
- What types of resources do students need?

Determine How to Scaffold the Close Read

- Who is doing the close reading?
- How many times do students revisit the text?
- Does any frontloading need to occur?
- How should the text be chunked?
- What types of annotations should be used?
- What types of student resources are needed?

We will consider each of these questions individually, plus a few more. However, it is important to remember that it is never possible to anticipate every twist in a dynamic classroom. The areas in which students struggle or make leaps will inform each lesson. The job of educators is to notice these areas and reactively adjust teaching in response. Table 3.1 (page 53) presents the elements of a close reading lesson in a format that highlights planning and decision making.

Table 3.1 Teaching Close Reading

Teaching

Limited Frontloading ☐ yes ☐ no
Describe:

First Read

Who Reads? ☐ teacher ☐ student

Student Materials

☐ graphic organizer   ☐ group consensus form

☐ note taking guide   ☐ summary form

Second Read

Who Reads? ☐ teacher ☐ student

Student Resources

☐ graphic organizer   ☐ group consensus form

☐ note taking guide   ☐ summary form

Additional Reads

Who Reads? ☐ teacher ☐ student

Student Resources

☐ graphic organizer   ☐ group consensus form

☐ note taking guide   ☐ summary form

Extension	Reteaching

Who Is Doing the Close Reading?

The first of the remaining lesson decisions is, perhaps deceptively, the most basic of all—who will be doing the actual reading? With those just beginning their journey as readers, the decision is easy. The teacher, being a fully fluent reader, reads the passage aloud at least for the first read, and if the students have not yet developed fluency, the teacher should do all of the reading. This provides students with the most information. It allows modeling of not only basic reading skills but also of the deeper questions that you are teaching them to generate. For these beginning readers, the close reading approach becomes a *close thinking* approach. Beginning readers may not have the technical skills to decode a complex piece of text, but they certainly have the thinking skills to notice and question challenging aspects of the writing.

More experienced students will tackle the text for the first time on their own. After all, one of the goals for the close reading approach is to create a challenge that forces students to productively struggle through worthy texts. There is, however, a place where the struggle can overcome the productivity. Sometimes, a text provides such a strong technical challenge that students can lose sight of the overall meaning of the passage. Or they become so distracted by an intellectual twist that they are unable to accurately focus on the themes or arguments. It may be possible to predict these issues based on your knowledge of your class and the specific text, or to uncover them while conducting formative assessments during the lesson. In either case, it may be productive to aid students in taking a step back to refocus on the pertinent parts of the text by choosing to read either a section or the entire text aloud yourself. In these cases, students, relieved of the duty to accurately decode, may consider other areas of interest in a rich piece of writing. Nuance and context that would be otherwise missed may materialize. Do not dismiss reading aloud if you believe it might meaningfully further the goals of the lesson.

How Many Times Do Students Revisit the Text?

The number of times students revisit each text is based on the lesson goals and the characteristics of the text. Some texts are sufficiently complex, challenging, and rewarding to merit spending several days with. Others may reveal the bulk of their mysteries after only two iterations of close reading. A text that is not complex enough to require reading more than once is unlikely to be a good candidate for this type of deep and detailed reading. A typical close reading will range from two to four sessions with a short, challenging text. Students must be given sufficient opportunity to engage in a productive struggle. Again, the goal is that every student in the class will gain full comprehension of these complex texts. There must be sufficient opportunity for each student to delve gradually deeper into the chosen reading.

It is critical to remain cognizant of students' engagement levels and avoid having the experience become rote or boring because of too many readings. Remember, each reread does not have to be of the entire text. A question you ask may involve rereading only a line or a paragraph. Rereadings are targeted as ways to conduct analysis of the word, sentence, paragraph, or text level. This is why text selection is an essential part of the close reading process. A properly chosen piece of text will not only be worthy of the scrutiny afforded during a close reading experience, but will also allow for the type of structured scaffolding that will draw in students of every level.

Does Any Frontloading Need to Occur?

After selecting the text, think about the knowledge demands needed for the piece. It is best, of course, if students can use context clues in the text to illuminate unfamiliar concepts and terms. For example, *The Great Kapok Tree* by Lynne Cherry is a richly complex text about the interconnectedness of life. Given the illustrations and context within the text, little or no frontloading is necessary to achieve deep comprehension. Unfamiliar animals and words can be determined through close reading and careful observation. However, sometimes it can be appropriate to frontload information that will provide necessary background knowledge for interpreting the text. *A New Coat for Anna* by Harriet Ziefert is a good example. It tells the story of a mother who goes to great lengths to get a coat for her daughter. It takes place in the aftermath of World War II when many businesses have closed and money is scarce. Students who have some general information about the impact of WWII will more fully comprehend the story. Consider pairing the close reading approach of texts that may have higher knowledge demands with, or subsequent to, other classroom activities surrounding that topic. If this is not possible, or if you choose to tackle a text with high knowledge demands that you are not confident all your students possess, insert the background information after students have interacted with the text during the first reading. Don't assume they do not know or they cannot do until they have been given an opportunity to try.

How Should the Text Be Chunked?

Chunking is a technique for dividing larger pieces of text into smaller, more manageable pieces. This makes it easier to cite a specific part of the text. A paragraph may be chunked into numbered sentences and phrases, with a longer text chunked into paragraphs and sections. Sometimes, a teacher may wish to pre-chunk the text for students. This has the advantage of saving class time and ensuring that everyone has an identical starting place. Other times, teachers may choose to have the class chunk the text together. This has the advantage of involving students with the text from the onset. If this is your choice, be sure that everyone has the same numbers for the same chunks. This is essential when referring to a particular chunk during classroom or group conversations.

By virtue of their necessarily short nature, close reading texts should not prove too daunting to chunk in any way you find preferable. In a truly short, single paragraph text, it would seem obvious to number each sentence or line. However, if the text is particularly challenging in its vocabulary and word choice, it may be more useful to chunk it by phrases so that individual words are easier to find. In a text with many short paragraphs, perhaps a lot of dialogue, paragraph chunking generally makes sense.

The main consideration is convenience. Balance the usefulness of easily identifying individual sentences or words with the amount of work it takes to number them and the amount of clutter the numbering might create on the page. At the heart of chunking are the text-dependent questions and their corresponding answers.

What Types of Annotations Should Be Used?

The ability for a reader to meaningfully interact with a text is enhanced and supported through text annotation. Text annotation enables students to engage with a text in a physical way, preventing them from skimming or discounting areas of challenge. However, random—though aesthetically pleasing—multi-colored highlights on a page do not add to the construction of meaning. In order for annotations to be useful, they must be consistent, and they must apply to the skills and standards being targeted. The way you approach annotation will depend on the age and skill level of your students and your own preferences. As long as the annotations are consistent and focused on the skills appropriate to your students, the variations are limitless. We encourage using a pencil so that the annotation can be accompanied by margin notes that later remind the student of what was meant by the annotation. For example, if the student puts a question mark next to a chunk, he should write the question in the margin. If a student circles a word, she should identify in the margin how the word is interesting or challenging.

Whatever the annotation, it is imperative to initially teach students the process of annotating. Once they are comfortable with this skill and the way to use it in your classroom, it will become an integral part of every close reading experience. Begin by introducing the standard marks students will use. See Table 3.2 (pages 58–59) for annotation ideas. Create and display a poster, defining these marks for easy reference. Also, provide students with a copy of the annotations chart to keep with their reading materials.

Chunking is meant to enable efficient references. Consider these two examples.

"In the ★ paragraph, the author begins calling the dog "Rusty" instead of "dog." Efficient paragraph chunking works well.

"In the ★ paragraph, in the—one, two, three, four, five—fifth sentence, the author uses the word "market." Inefficient—chunking by line or sentence would be better.

Name: _____ Date: _____

Bobbing Daisies

¹ I love a field of daisies
Bobbing in the sun,
Gently tucking in their heads
When the day is done.

² I say, "Good night, daisies!"
And "Good night, sun!"
Then bob with daisies in my dreams
When the day is done.

112 51540—Dive into Close Reading

examples of
chunked text

Name: _____ Date: _____

Dear Mayor Keen

¹ Dear Mayor Keen,

² I am writing to ask the city to open a dog park. During the day, my dog stays in the house. At night, we take walks. But we always need to keep him on a leash. There are no places for him to run freely. This makes me sad. Dogs are happiest when they can scamper and play fetch. They love to race each other. I know my dog misses jogging in the grass. His tail barely wags. If we had a park with a fence, the dogs here could run and play. They would be healthier and happier.

³ Please let me know what you think!

⁴ Sincerely,

⁵ Oscar Trent and Spot

Dog Behavior

¹ Dogs like to play. They chase balls and toys.

² They pretend to hunt. They wrestle with each other.

³ Puppies jump, run, and pounce when they play.

⁴ Sometimes, they get rough. But when they are done, they cuddle.

246 51540—Dive into Close Reading

© Shell Education

Table 3.2 Annotation Ideas

Grades K–1

	Annotation	When Do I Use It?
Author's Message	main idea	This is the big idea.
Author's Craft	√	I found it! (e.g., title page, table of contents, or graph)
Questions	?	What does this mean? or I have a question.
Opinions	!	Wow! I am surprised! or I think this is important!
Language	(unknown word)	I don't know this word.
Connections	1⟵⟶2	This goes with this.
Reflections and Predictions	(shared orally)	These are thoughts I had while reading. and I think this will happen next.

Grade 2

	Annotation	When Do I Use It?
Author's Message	main idea	This is the theme or main idea.
Author's Craft	√	I found it! (e.g., title page, table of contents, or graph)
Questions	?	I don't understand. or I have a question.
	*	I should find out more about this.
Opinions	!	Wow! I am surprised! or I think this is important!
Language	(unknown word)	I don't know this word.
	figurative language	Examples: metaphor, simile, idiom, multiple-meaning word, nonliteral word, personification, alliteration, hyperbole, or onomatopoeia
Connections	1⟷2	This goes with this. or This leads to this. or These are connected somehow.
Reflections and Prediction	margin notes	These are thoughts I had while reading. and I think this will happen next.
Arguments	(What the author says is true)	When the author is making an argument or important statement
	goes against the author's argument	This goes against the author's argument or main idea.

Next, model your thinking for students as you read a piece of text aloud. Explain that the annotations help you return to a text to clarify questions, research confusing words, focus on important features, and make connections between sections of the text. Have students practice annotating the same text you read aloud. Then, invite them to try it on their own with a new piece of text. Once they have had some time to annotate, encourage peer discussion of the annotations. Finally, reconvene the class to make sure everyone understands and is consistently using the same symbols. As the class becomes more adept with using annotation tools, feel free to experiment by adding more symbols, if needed.

Before beginning each close reading experience, determine the types of annotations that may be needed. For example, if it is a lesson centering on challenging language, remind students to focus on annotating unfamiliar words or words used in unfamiliar ways. For lessons about key ideas and details, students might focus on underlining phrases that indicate the key ideas and circling those that provide supporting details. Not every type of annotation must be used in each lesson. Annotations are only useful inasmuch as they support students' learning goals and needs. Students should, however, be encouraged to use the annotations that support their engagement with the text.

What Types of Student Resources Are Needed?

Each close reading experience requires that students have a text to read and tools to annotate their reading. However, as you plan, consider what other types of materials will maximize the close reading experience for students, such as graphic organizers. There may be times when additional support is needed, such as partnered texts, appropriate realia, maps, illustrations, or even partnered multi-media presentations. These scaffolds should, however, not be introduced until students have completed an initial read of the text.

Teacher Tip

Annotations may be done by writing directly on the text, employing the use of sticky notes, or using clear page protectors over book pages and using dry erase markers to annotate.

Bear in mind that formative assessments may reveal areas where certain students may benefit from scaffolded support. One cannot always anticipate what supports will be needed, but it is helpful to have options in mind when lesson planning. For example, inviting students who are struggling with the text into a smaller group to review challenging vocabulary is one form of scaffolding. Having in mind the types of scaffolds you will use with a group to support vocabulary or conceptual development eases any worries caused by having to think of scaffolds on the spot.

Finally, provide a summative performance task to assess mastery of skills taught for this lesson. The task should prompt students to use writing, speaking, or creating to demonstrate their new understanding. Sample performance tasks are provided in Section Four. Plus, lesson-specific organizers are offered with each sample lesson in Section Five. While the larger group starts this task, you can work with the smaller group to ready them for eventual completion of the extension task. Remember that working with a small group does not mean they are excluded from the reading of the complex text or the extension task. The goal is to ensure they have additional opportunities to gain the language and concepts needed to also move forward.

Putting It All Together

Let's return to Mrs. Mohr's first grade class for a model of how a close reading lesson might play out. Before the lesson, Mrs. Mohr has completed the planning chart and considered the text complexity of the passage for her lesson.

During the close reading lesson, Mrs. Mohr briefly introduces the purpose and sets expectations. She presents the text with numbers or symbols next to each "chunk." She reviews a few relevant annotation marks and presents a broad text-dependent question before having students listen to her read the text or, when appropriate, read the text themselves.

As students review the words and pictures, Mrs. Mohr becomes a facilitator. She rereads portions of the text and guides students to write, draw, or dictate their annotations. Because of her flexibility and planning, Mrs. Mohr is able to offer timely words of encouragement and additional guiding questions where needed. She adds to partner conversations and pulls the whole class together for discussion and continued guiding questions as needed. Simultaneously, Mrs. Mohr is an active observer. She documents students' successes, students' struggles, students' responses to scaffolds, and skills with which students need more instruction.

The class completes several phases of reading and interacting with text-dependent questions in mind, discussing with partners, discussing with the whole class, and considering new questions and prompts. With each phase, the students discover deeper meaning, and the teacher crafts specific responses to observed needs. These phases may take place in one session or across two to three sessions spread over a couple of days. Multiply this experience across a school year and across content areas, and students will build foundations that will help them confront complex texts.

Lesson Resource Checklist

❑ Pre-chunked/numbered text or text ready to be chunked

❑ Student-friendly lesson purpose posted where students can see and refer to it

❑ "I Can" statement that matches the lesson purpose

❑ Annotation tools (e.g., pencils, sticky notes, page protectors, or dry erase markers)

❑ Text-dependent questions

❑ Graphic organizers

❑ Scaffolding tools (e.g., partner text, realia, maps, or illustrations)

❑ Formative performance task

Try It!

Directions: Return to the passage you analyzed on page 50. Use the guidelines and tables in this section along with your knowledge of your students to prepare a close reading lesson. Write on the chart on the next page, or use the digital copy of the chart from the Digital Download (teachingclosereading.pdf).

Make sure to tab or mark the pages you find most helpful to your work. These are the pages to which you can return when you plan actual lessons to use with your students.

Pretty in Pink (Lexile 570L)

Just when we think we've seen it all, along comes a giant pink surprise!

Park rangers in Australia have made a big discovery. They found large pink slugs that no one knew existed. But this slug species has been around for millions of years. It lives only on Mount Kaputar in Australia. Most of the time the slugs stay hidden. But they come out after big rainstorms.

Australia was once covered in rainforests. But that was long ago. Much of Australia is dry now. Mount Kaputar is unique. Plants there are thick and colorful. Some living things that have died out everywhere else still live well there. The pink slug is one of those lucky animals.

The slug is about eight inches long. That makes it about twice the size of most other slugs. Its bright pink color helps it stay hidden among colorful leaves.

But the pink beauties are not the only new things the forest rangers found! They also spied three new species of snails. But these aren't just any snails. Oh, no! These snails are cannibals! They eat their own kind. These creepy creatures follow the trail left by other snails. And then, lunchtime!

Whether they are big and pink or creepy cannibals, no one will think of slugs and snails in the same way again!

Teaching Close Reading

Teaching

Limited Frontloading ☐ yes ☐ no
Describe:

First Read

Who Reads? ☐ teacher ☐ student

Student Materials

☐ graphic organizer   ☐ group consensus form

☐ note taking guide   ☐ summary form

Second Read

Who Reads? ☐ teacher ☐ student

Student Resources

☐ graphic organizer   ☐ group consensus form

☐ note taking guide   ☐ summary form

Additional Reads

Who Reads? ☐ teacher ☐ student

Student Resources

☐ graphic organizer   ☐ group consensus form

☐ note taking guide   ☐ summary form

Extension	**Reteaching**

Section 4:
Assessing and Extending Close Reading

One cannot be certain what students have learned or are learning until there is an assessment given. Formative assessments are used to inform instruction throughout the learning process. A formative assessment is an assessment *for* learning, not *of* learning. It provides a snapshot of where the students' development is during a particular point in time. Assessment is a continual process that occurs throughout close reading. As you engage with your students, you will repeatedly assess their learning and scaffold accordingly. However, it is quite useful to have built-in checkpoints for formative assessments at specific times during your lesson. "I Can" statements provide an avenue for students to assess their own learning. Stating what he or she can do in relation to the learning targets builds student ownership of learning and self-efficacy. It is also encouraged to have formal performance tasks at the end of a close reading lesson. These performance tasks serve as summative assessments, which are good ways to gauge the outcome of your students' close reading. We have included formative and summative assessments with each of the sample lessons included in the Literary Text Close Reading Lessons (page 76).

Figure 4.1 presents the Planning Chart for Close Reading introduced in Section Two. In this section, we will address the last two elements.

Figure 4.1 Planning Chart for Close Reading

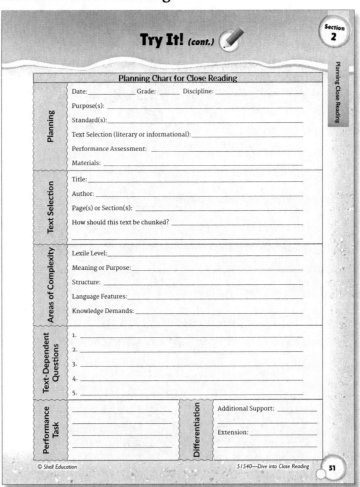

Creating and Using Formative Assessments

As students participate in close reading, there will be numerous opportunities for you to observe, probe, and evaluate student learning. The two biggest keys to making effective use of formative assessments are noticing the areas of challenge and anticipating the flexibility needed in planning to address the next areas of challenge as the lesson progresses.

Assessing What You Hear

Partner talk and table talk during a close reading lesson provides rich data to monitor and assess student learning. As students discuss the text and text-dependent questions, listen carefully for indications of understanding or confusion. Engage with student pairs and groups to support their discussions and ask follow-up questions that spur students to dig deeper. If it is clear one student is dominating the conversation, pose a question to the other student. If students seem to be struggling unproductively or showing a lack of understanding, make a notation and be ready to scaffold or reteach. It is not necessary to leap to the rescue of struggling students, but it is important to remain aware of problem areas and structure the lessons to offer scaffolds that promote continued learning. When problems persist, students may lose focus or fall behind, so it is important to remember that the goal of the close reading approach is for *every* student to be able to tackle and successfully read increasingly complex, challenging, age-appropriate texts.

Assessing What You See

As students work through annotating their texts and producing written reactions on their graphic organizers, you will have another opportunity to assess their understanding. Once again, it is important to tune in to the students' work and evaluate strengths and growth areas. Are the same instances of challenging vocabulary coming up on many students' annotations? Are all students clearly able to identify the main idea and supporting details of the text, recording them accurately on their graphic organizers? Are students' paired discussions focused and on target? Are there instances of figurative language causing unanticipated challenges? Are there repeated questions coming up in students' margin notes? Look carefully at what students are annotating, and carefully consider students' written responses to text-dependent questions.

Text-Dependent Question Observation Guides

Your assessment of what is seen and heard must directly relate to the lesson's goals. Creating pertinent, probing text-dependent questions is essential. Once students are focused on well-considered TDQs and you are engaged in listening and seeing students' progress and struggles, you will need an efficient, organized way to keep track of your observations. Table 4.1 (pages 66–68) offers two observational guides—one for literature and one for informational text—to assist you in quickly recording what you see and hear in terms of the students' mastery of the meaning, structure, language, and knowledge demands of the text.

Table 4.1 Observation Guides

Observation Guide (Literary Text)				
	Meaning	**Structure**	**Language**	**Knowledge Demands**
1st Reading Notes	❏ main idea ❏ key details ❏ vocabulary word use ❏ development of characters or themes	❏ macro (overall) organization ❏ micro (sentence/ paragraph) organization ❏ visual supports ❏ relationship among ideas and vocabulary ❏ relationship among ideas, characters, and setting	❏ vocabulary word meaning ❏ unconventional jargon, vernacular, or technical terminology ❏ author purpose ❏ point of view ❏ theme	❏ cultural or historical knowledge ❏ literary knowledge ❏ technical knowledge
2nd Reading Notes	❏ main idea ❏ key details ❏ vocabulary word use ❏ development of characters or themes	❏ macro (overall) organization ❏ micro (sentence/ paragraph) organization ❏ visual supports ❏ relationship among ideas and vocabulary ❏ relationship among ideas, characters, and setting	❏ vocabulary word meaning ❏ unconventional jargon, vernacular, or technical terminology ❏ author purpose ❏ point of view ❏ theme	❏ cultural or historical knowledge ❏ literary knowledge ❏ technical knowledge

Observation Guide (Literary Text)

	Meaning	Structure	Language	Knowledge Demands
3rd Reading Notes	❑ main idea ❑ key details ❑ vocabulary word use ❑ development of characters or themes	❑ macro (overall) organization ❑ micro (sentence/ paragraph) organization ❑ visual supports ❑ relationship among ideas and vocabulary ❑ relationship among ideas, characters, and setting	❑ vocabulary word meaning ❑ unconventional jargon, vernacular, or technical terminology ❑ author purpose ❑ point of view ❑ theme	❑ cultural or historical knowledge ❑ literary knowledge ❑ technical knowledge
4th Reading Notes	❑ main idea ❑ key details ❑ vocabulary word use ❑ development of characters or themes	❑ macro (overall) organization ❑ micro (sentence/ paragraph) organization ❑ visual supports ❑ relationship among ideas and vocabulary ❑ relationship among ideas, characters, and setting	❑ vocabulary word meaning ❑ unconventional jargon, vernacular, or technical terminology ❑ author purpose ❑ point of view ❑ theme	❑ cultural or historical knowledge ❑ literary knowledge ❑ technical knowledge

Table 4.1 Observation Guides *(cont.)*

Observation Guide (Informational Text)

	Meaning	Structure	Language	Knowledge Demands
1st Reading Notes	❑ main idea ❑ key details ❑ vocabulary word use	❑ macro (overall) organization ❑ micro (sentence/ paragraph) organization ❑ visual supports ❑ relationship among ideas and vocabulary	❑ vocabulary word meaning ❑ idioms ❑ unconventional jargon, vernacular, or technical terminology ❑ author's purpose	❑ cultural or historical knowledge ❑ discipline-based knowledge ❑ technical knowledge
2nd Reading Notes	❑ main idea ❑ key details ❑ vocabulary word use	❑ macro (overall) organization ❑ micro (sentence/ paragraph) organization ❑ visual supports ❑ relationship among ideas and vocabulary	❑ vocabulary word meaning ❑ idioms ❑ unconventional jargon, vernacular, or technical terminology ❑ author's purpose	❑ cultural or historical knowledge ❑ discipline-based knowledge ❑ technical knowledge
3rd Reading Notes	❑ main idea ❑ key details ❑ vocabulary word use	❑ macro (overall) organization ❑ micro (sentence/ paragraph) organization ❑ visual supports ❑ relationship among ideas and vocabulary	❑ vocabulary word meaning ❑ idioms ❑ unconventional jargon, vernacular, or technical terminology ❑ author's purpose	❑ cultural or historical knowledge ❑ discipline-based knowledge ❑ technical knowledge
4th Reading Notes	❑ main idea ❑ key details ❑ vocabulary word use	❑ macro (overall) organization ❑ micro (sentence/ paragraph) organization ❑ visual supports ❑ relationship among ideas and vocabulary	❑ vocabulary word meaning ❑ idioms ❑ unconventional jargon, vernacular, or technical terminology ❑ author's purpose	❑ cultural or historical knowledge ❑ discipline-based knowledge ❑ technical knowledge

To use an observational guide, attach it to a clipboard or carry it in a convenient place while walking around the room during annotation times, partner talks, or class discussions. Record students' first names or initials to the left of the topics with which they are demonstrating mastery and to the right of those topics with which they are struggling. After the first reading, you may not wish to take any action unless there is a glaring problem that students seem unable or unwilling to work through. However, if after observing the second or third readings, it is obvious that the same students are continuing to wrestle with the same issues or if a growing number of students are grappling with the same issue, it may be time to intervene. Figure 4.2 provides a sample of a completed guide from Mrs. Thom's classroom.

Figure 4.2 Completed Sample Observation Guide

Literary Text Observation Guide

	Meaning	Structure	Language	Knowledge Demands
1st Reading Notes and Comments Whole class discussion on language and details	☐ main idea ☑ key details ☐ vocabulary word use ☐ development of characters or themes groups 3+5	☐ macro (overall) organization ☐ micro (sentence/paragraph) organization ☐ visual layout ☐ visual supports ☐ relationship among ideas and vocabulary ☐ relationship among ideas, characters, and setting	☑ vocabulary word meaning *Izzy, Jose, Dan, TC, Ronnie* ☑ idioms ☐ unconventional jargon, vernacular, or technical terminology ☐ tone ☐ author purpose *Jessie, Leslie, Latisha, Phil* ☑ figurative language ☐ point of view ☐ theme	☑ cultural or historical knowledge ☐ literary knowledge ☐ technical knowledge
2nd Reading Notes and Comments To Do: Small group focus on Vocab @ idioms Group 3 work on details	☐ main idea ☐ key details *group 3* ☐ vocabulary word use ☐ development of characters or themes w/7	☐ macro (overall) organization ☐ micro (sentence/paragraph) organization ☐ visual layout ☐ visual supports ☐ relationship among ideas and vocabulary ☐ relationship among ideas, characters, and setting	☑ vocabulary word meaning ☑ idioms ☐ unconventional jargon, vernacular, or technical terminology ☐ tone *Dan, Izzy, Jose, Jessie, Leslie* ☐ author purpose ☑ figurative language ☐ point of view ☐ theme	☑ cultural or historical knowledge *Johan?* ☐ literary knowledge ☐ technical knowledge
3rd Reading Notes and Comments on with Izzy	☐ main idea ☑ key details ☐ vocabulary word use ☐ development of characters or themes Izzy	☐ macro (overall) organization ☐ micro (sentence/paragraph) organization ☐ visual layout ☐ visual supports ☐ relationship among ideas and vocabulary ☐ relationship among ideas, characters, and setting	☑ vocabulary word meaning *Izzy* ☐ idioms ☐ unconventional jargon, vernacular, or technical terminology ☐ tone ☐ author purpose ☐ figurative language ☐ point of view ☐ theme	☐ cultural or historical knowledge ☐ literary knowledge ☐ technical knowledge
4th Reading Notes and Comments Great!	☐ main idea ☐ key details ☐ vocabulary word use ☐ development of characters or themes	☐ macro (overall) organization ☐ micro (sentence/paragraph) organization ☐ visual layout ☐ visual supports ☐ relationship among ideas and vocabulary ☐ relationship among ideas, characters, and setting	☐ vocabulary word meaning ☐ idioms ☐ unconventional jargon, vernacular, or technical terminology ☐ tone ☐ author purpose ☐ figurative language ☐ point of view ☐ theme	☐ cultural or historical knowledge ☐ literary knowledge ☐ technical knowledge

The completed sample observation guide (Figure 4.2) is taken from Mrs. Thom's second grade classroom that engaged in a literary text close reading, focusing on key ideas and details. The students sit in heterogeneous table groups for discussion and collaborative work. Groups are discussing the question, "What details show how the main character changed throughout the story?" As Mrs. Thom moves around the room while listening to the discussions, she realizes that several students are not clear on some of the language in the complex text. She notes specific students and/or table groups and the exact problematic language. Additionally, two groups focus on unimportant details in the text. Mrs. Thom attempts to refocus the groups by asking them which details are important for understanding the main character. After listening to the groups for a while longer, she determines that it is a good time to have a whole-class discussion about the specific language used in the text and how the details relate to the main character. She notes that decision on her observation guide.

Once again, during the second reading, Mrs. Thom leads a whole-group discussion. It is clear that significantly more students are understanding the text. There are still a few of her students who are new to English and who are wrestling with the more complex vocabulary and figurative language. Additionally, Johan, who seemed clear before, asks a question that makes Mrs. Thom wonder if he is trying to be funny or has actually become confused. She puts a question mark (?) next to his name to remind her to check in with him later. Students in Table Group 5 are now progressing without issue. But students in Table Group 3 are still focusing on insignificant details. Mrs. Thom decides to have the class work together to annotate her displayed copy of the text as a model for the students who are continuing to struggle.

During the third reading, Mrs. Thom is happy to see that almost all of the students understand the text. However, Izzy is still unable to identify the key details and language. Mrs. Thom makes a note to work with Izzy one-on-one.

Because of the individual and small-group scaffolds Mrs. Thom offers, each student has the opportunity to be as independent as possible, struggle appropriately, then receive the level of support he or she needs to be successful. Mrs. Thom is ready to move students on to their formative assessments.

Creating and Using Summative Assessments— The Performance Task

Summative assessments are used at the end of a series of lessons to determine what learning has taken place. They let the teacher and students know what was learned as the result of the close reading experiences. It gives students the opportunity to demonstrate their learning and teachers the chance to evaluate whether any additional instruction is needed. For the purposes of the close reading approach, performance tasks that are based on learning goals are the summative assessments used. These tasks reflect the knowledge gained through students' experiences with the text-dependent questions. There are an endless number of performance tasks that can be chosen for students. Certain tasks, however, lend themselves better to certain age levels and goals. See Table 4.2 (page 71) for some suggested performance tasks at various grade levels.

Table 4.2 Sample Performance Tasks

Grade Level	Sample Performance Tasks
Kindergarten	• Students, with prompting and support from the teacher, describe the key events of the text. • Students create images of the main character, including key details from the text. • With support from the teacher, students retell the main events of the text in order. • Students demonstrate understanding of the text by participating in the activity it describes. • Students role-play scenes or parts of the text. • Students create storyboards showing the main events of a text.
1st	• Students differentiate the points at which various characters are telling the story by highlighting each character's narration in a distinct color. • Students analyze the text to identify words and phrases that contribute to the feelings they experience when reading it and use these words to create their own sentences. • With prompting and support from the teacher, students create pictures of the setting, including details from the text. • Students produce a collaborative poster, explaining character development/changes (for a literature text) or a public service announcement or awareness poster (for an informational text). • Students prepare skits, role-playing characters from the story in a different setting.
2nd	• Students create reader's theater scripts from the text and perform them for the class. • Students create dialogues between two characters from the text/story, demonstrating the differences in their points of view. • After identifying the *who*, *what*, *where*, *when*, and *why* of the text or story, students exchange the *where* for one of their own choosing and summarize the story with the new information. • Students create posters demonstrating the cause and effect of the main events of the text. • Students create problem-solution posters for an informational text (e.g., too much carbon in the air from cars on the road or grocery bags in the Pacific Ocean). • Students compare the setting of two different texts by creating split dioramas.

What Should I Do for Students Who Comprehend at the End of Close Reading?

If the summative assessment indicates that students have completely comprehended the material used in the close reading, outstanding! Your students were able to accomplish the intended purpose. For them, it is time to move forward. Bear in mind that they now have a bit more experience and a bit more success upon which to draw as you plan future lessons. They are in better positions to push just a little further with the next close reading experience. The process should never be stagnant. Each time this approach is utilized, it's like shooting for the sweet spot where students are engaged, challenged, and capable of growth. If the challenges are too few, students will not have opportunities to stretch and learn. They may even become bored. Think back to the formative evaluations. If students sailed through without any struggle, it may be necessary to rethink your challenge level for the next close reading lesson. Return to the description of text complexity in Section Two, and choose an element to amp up.

How Do I Extend Learning for Students Who Did Not Understand?

If some students are still struggling and not showing mastery of the lesson purpose through their performance tasks, it is time to plan how to move them forward by considering what and how to reteach. Remember, the goal of every close reading experience is for *each* student, including those who read below grade level and English language learners, to show deep comprehension of challenging grade-level texts. When this goal is not reached, it is necessary to identify problem areas and scaffold their learning until they reach the targeted goals.

What Makes for a Good Performance Task?

- It aligns with the standards being taught.
- It utilizes a format that enables students with various language and reading proficiencies to demonstrate knowledge.
- It targets a high level of Bloom's Taxonomy/Depth of Knowledge.
- Optional: It incorporates STEM features to broaden appeal and experience.

There are many ways to support students who struggle. Table 4.3 (page 73) offers specific options for reteaching. You may incorporate a reteaching option during a close reading lesson in response to your observations. Alternatively, you may record the need for reteaching, then use the reteach option during the next close reading lesson. See the Glossary of Reteaching Ideas (page 264) for explanations of each reteaching idea.

Table 4.3 Reteaching Ideas

Identified Area for Growth	Reteaching Ideas	
Vocabulary	• Frayer cards • word maps • graphic organizers • word sorts • T-chart	• words in context • vocabulary matrices • personal dictionaries • connect two
Key Details	• Gimme 5 • graphic organizers	• concept maps
Main Idea	• concept maps • tweet the main idea	• newspaper headlines and story titles
Plot Structure	• storyboards • Freytag's Pyramid • plot skeleton	• Somebody Wanted But So Then (SWBST) • story summary graphic organizers
Text Structure	• graphic organizers • character web • story maps	• task cards • signal terms
Character Analysis	• graphic organizers • character web	• Venn diagrams • character profiles
Text Features	• text feature BINGO • text feature checklist	• graphic organizers
Theme	• graphic organizers • essential questions	• hash tags • task cards
Figurative Language	• graphic organizers • song lyrics	• task cards
Tone & Mood	• graphic organizers • essential questions • task cards	• flip-flop • inquiry charts
Opinion/Argument Development	• graphic organizers • task cards	• Toulmin Model of Arguments • claim/evidence/analysis
Reading Visuals	• Somebody Wanted But So Then (SWBST) • graphic organizers	• task cards • Visual Thinking Strategies (VTS)

Try It!

Directions: Return to the close reading plans you created on page 63. Use the guidelines and tables in this section along with your knowledge of your students to create a performance task and prepare for observation and reteaching. Write on the chart on page 75, or use the digital copy of the chart from the Digital Download (planningclosereading.pdf).

Make sure to tab or mark the pages you find most helpful to your work. These are the pages to which you can return when you plan actual lessons to use with your students.

Pretty in Pink (Lexile 570L)

Just when we think we've seen it all, along comes a giant pink surprise!

Park rangers in Australia have made a big discovery. They found large pink slugs that no one knew existed. But this slug species has been around for millions of years. It lives only on Mount Kaputar in Australia. Most of the time the slugs stay hidden. But they come out after big rainstorms.

Australia was once covered in rainforests. But that was long ago. Much of Australia is dry now. Mount Kaputar is unique. Plants there are thick and colorful. Some living things that have died out everywhere else still live well there. The pink slug is one of those lucky animals.

The slug is about eight inches long. That makes it about twice the size of most other slugs. Its bright pink color helps it stay hidden among colorful leaves.

But the pink beauties are not the only new things the forest rangers found! They also spied three new species of snails. But these aren't just any snails. Oh, no! These snails are cannibals! They eat their own kind. These creepy creatures follow the trail left by other snails. And then, lunchtime!

Whether they are big and pink or creepy cannibals, no one will think of slugs and snails in the same way again!

Try It!

Planning Chart for Close Reading

Planning

Date:_____ Grade: _____ Discipline: _____

Purpose(s): _____

Standard(s):_____

Text Selection (literary or informational):_____

Performance Assessment: _____

Materials: _____

Text Selection

Title:_____

Author: _____

Page(s) or Section(s): _____

How should this text be chunked? _____

_____

Areas of Complexity

Lexile Level:_____

Meaning or Purpose:_____

Structure: _____

Language Features:_____

Knowledge Demands: _____

Text-Dependent Questions

1. _____

2. _____

3. _____

4. _____

5. _____

Performance Task

_____

_____

_____

_____

Differentiation

Additional Support: _____

_____

Extension: _____

_____

Section 5:
Literary Text Close Reading Lessons

If you have completed the Try It! activities at the end of each of the previous sections, you now have a planned close reading lesson that you may choose to use with your students. You also have a set of tabbed pages to refer to as you plan additional lessons. In this section, you will find a bank of sample close reading lessons. You may choose to use the actual lesson (all of the passages and resources are provided) or use them as models as you create lessons.

You will find nine close reading lessons built around literary texts. A tenth text is provided along with planning resources to allow you to plan a close reading lesson.

Key Ideas and Details Kindergarten Lesson 77

Key Ideas and Details Grade 1 Lesson 87

Key Ideas and Details Grade 2 Lesson 97

Craft and Structure Kindergarten Lesson 107

Craft and Structure Grade 1 Lesson 117

Craft and Structure Grade 2 Lesson. 127

Integration of Knowledge and Ideas Kindergarten Lesson 137

Integration of Knowledge and Ideas Grade 1 Lesson 147

Integration of Knowledge and Ideas Grade 2 Lesson. 157

Try It! 166

The Ninja's Surpise

Purpose

WHAT: Analyze the actions of characters in a story and predict future actions.

HOW: Draw a picture of what the characters will do in the future.

I CAN: I can predict actions of characters in a story.

Standards

→ **Reading:** With guidance and support, make inferences regarding the actions of characters in a story.

→ **Writing:** With guidance and support, draw, write, or dictate an answer to a question using information from a provided source.

→ **Language:** With guidance and support, produce simple sentences in response to a prompt.

Performance Assessment

→ Students will draw pictures of what a character will do in the future.

Text Selection

→ "The Ninja's Surprise"

→ Text is organized in paragraphs.

Materials

→ *The Ninja's Surprise* passage, one copy per student (page 82; ninjassurprise.pdf)

→ *Act Like a Princess* activity (page 83)

→ *He'll Be Back* activity (page 84)

→ *He'll Be Back Reflection Page* (page 85)

Text-Dependent Questions (See pages 40–42 for more information.)

→ What is this story about?

→ Who are the characters?

→ What can you tell about the ninja by how he is acting?

→ What can you tell about the princess by how she is acting?

→ Why is the title "The Ninja's Surprise"?

The Ninja's Surpise *(cont.)*

Areas of Complexity

	Measure	Explanation
Quantitative	Lexile Level	350L
Qualitative	Meaning or Purpose	The text relates the sequence of events of a ninja's mission and what happens next. Key details about the characters are not stated explicitly. The reader must make an inference to fully understand the meaning.
	Structure	The passage is a narrative with an ordered sequence of events.
	Language Features	The passage contains vocabulary that is sophisticated and precise that may interfere with understanding of the overall plot. Knowledge about ninjas is necessary to fully understand the story.
Reader/ Task	Knowledge Demands	Inferences must be made in order to comprehend the story. Students must understand the character and predict his actions to complete the performance task.

Text Synopsis

A ninja sneaks into a castle to steal a ring that a princess is wearing. The princess wakes up from a deep sleep to find the ninja in her room. She springs into action, attacking the ninja with her own ninja-like moves. As soon as she does, a black bird, the sign of a ninja spy group, swoops down. The ninja flees the castle confused; however, he is determined to return.

Differentiation

Additional Support—Provide students with practice making everyday inferences. Provide two clues and ask students what conclusion they can draw, for example, "I smell something good. My stomach is growling. It can be inferred that I am hungry."

Extension—Show students a picture. Ask them to state two facts they can tell by looking at the picture and to make two inferences from the picture.

The Ninja's Surpise (cont.)

Phase 1—Hitting the Surface

Who Reads | **Annotations (See page 58.)**

☑ teacher   ☑ highlight main points   ☐ underline key details   ☐ write questions

☐ students   ☑ circle key vocabulary   ☐ arrows for connections   ☐ other: _____

Procedure

1. Tell students that they will listen to a story several times. Each time will be for a different purpose, to gain a better understanding of the story.

2. Display a copy of "The Ninja's Surprise" (page 82). Have students listen as you read the passage to get an overall idea of the story.

3. Ask students, "What is this story about? Who are the characters?"

4. **Partners**—After students have listened to you read the story once, ask partners to briefly retell the story using the correct sequence of events.

5. **Whole Class**—Regroup as a class, and display the text for all students. Ask students to share their responses to the two initial questions. Make annotations on your copy of the text.

Phase 2—Digging Deeper

Who Reads | **Annotations (See page 58.)**

☑ teacher   ☐ highlight main points   ☑ underline key details   ☐ write questions

☐ students   ☐ circle key vocabulary   ☐ arrows for connections   ☐ other: _____

Procedure

1. Remind students that readers make inferences when they discover what the author means without the author saying it directly. Tell students that during this reading, they are going to dig deeper into the actions of the characters.

2. Display a copy of the text, and read only the first sentence. Guide students to make an inference about the ninja using the first sentence by asking, "What can you tell about the ninja by how he is acting?"

Phase 2—Digging Deeper *(cont.)*

Procedure *(cont.)*

3. If needed, ask additional layered/scaffolded questions, such as:
   - What is the ninja doing?
   - Why would he act that way?
   - Why is he hiding?
   - Why is he staying in the shadow?
   - What is someone who is hiding and staying in shadows trying to do?

4. **Partners**—Reread the next two sentences in the paragraph. Stop after each sentence, and have students discuss the question with partners, "What can you tell about the ninja by how he is acting?"

5. If needed, support students with the vocabulary words *swiftly* and *darted* by modeling how to move in those ways in order to help them better understand the sentence.

6. **Whole Class**—Gather together as a class, and display the text for all students. Ask students to share their responses to the question about the ninja. Record the textual evidence for their responses with annotations on the displayed copy of the text. Ask students:
   - Do all three sentences help the reader understand that the ninja is sneaking into the castle?
   - What words in each sentence help the reader know more about the ninja?

7. Reread the first paragraph one last time. Have students act out the paragraph as you read it slowly. Their actions should model the words used in the text and the inference they have made about the ninja being sneaky.

Phase 3—Going Even Deeper

Who Reads	Annotations (See page 58.)		
☑ teacher	☐ highlight main points	☑ underline key details	☐ write questions
☐ students	☑ circle key vocabulary	☐ arrows for connections	☐ other: _____

Procedure

1. Ask students what they remember about the characters in the story.

2. This time as you read, they will dig in deeper to learn more about the princess. Display a copy of the text. Reread paragraphs 4, 5, and 6. Ask students to think about the same question they did for the ninja. "What can you tell about the princess by how she is acting?"

Phase 3—Going Even Deeper *(cont.)*

Procedure *(cont.)*

3. Model annotating the text by underlining as students identify key details about what the princess is doing.

4. Ask students to complete the *Act Like a Princess* activity (page 83) to compare the princess from this story to the princesses from other stories.

5. **Partners**—Allow students to share their work with each other and to discuss the differences between the two drawings.

6. Continue reading the remainder of the text. Ask students to identify any vocabulary they do not understand. Annotate the text by circling the vocabulary that students identify.

   • Students will likely not understand the reference to the *Choho Clan*. Explain to students that they can often figure out vocabulary from the story. Say, "I see the words are capitalized. I know names start with capital letters. What does *Choho Clan* name? What do you know about the *Choho Clan* from the story?"

7. **Partners**—After students have listened to you read the text again, encourage them to discuss and provide text-based evidence for the following questions.

   • What is the black bird a sign of?
   • When does it appear?
   • How does the ninja feel about the bird?
   • Why does the bird appear right after the princess attacks the ninja?
   • Who belongs to the Choho Clan? How do you know?

8. **Whole Class**—Ask students to discuss the question *Why is the title "The Ninja's Surprise"?* Encourage students to support their inferences using evidence from the text.

Performance Assessment

1. Assign the performance task *He'll Be Back* (page 84).

2. Guide students to think about their work and complete the *He'll Be Back Reflection Page* (page 85).

The Ninja's Surprise

1   The ninja hid in the shadow of a tree. He waited until a cloud passed in front of the moon. Swiftly, he darted up the castle's wall until he found his target.

2   He eyed the sleeping princess. This was going to be easier than he had thought. The princess rolled over. There was the ring. Focused on his mission, he crept forward.

3   Silently, he reached for the ring.

4   The princess snored.

5   He closed his hand around her finger. He would not fail his master.

6   Suddenly, the princess leapt from the floor. Her foot made contact with his leg. She grabbed his arm and flipped him on to the floor.

7   "The ring is mine!" she screamed. A black bird swooped down from the sky. It was the sign of the Choho Clan.

8   Shocked, the ninja threw a firecracker into the room and darted through the window.

9   He understood little. But he knew he would be back.

Act Like a Princess

Directions: Draw a picture on each side.

How a Princess Usually Acts

How the Princess in the Story Acts

He'll Be Back

Directions: Draw a picture. Show what the ninja will do when he comes back to the castle. Then, finish the sentence.

The ninja will _____ .

Note: Students may dictate their sentences to the teacher.

He'll Be Back Reflection Page

Directions: Think about your work. Did you follow directions? Circle the *thumbs up* or *thumbs down* picture for each part.

What I Think about My Work

	Yes	No
I showed what the ninja will do.	👍	👎
My sentence matches my drawing.	👍	👎

Teacher comments: _____

_____

_____

_____

_____

_____

_____

Rubric based on work by Lapp, D., B. Moss, M. Grant, & K. Johnson (2015)

The Boy Who Loved Books

Purpose

WHAT: Understand how a character changes in a story.

HOW: Draw a picture and write/dictate a sentence showing how a character changed.

I CAN: I can describe how a character changes in a story.

Standards

→ **Reading:** Answer questions about key details.

→ **Writing:** Write to describe how a character changes in a text.

→ **Language:** Use context clues to determine the meaning of words and phrases.

Performance Assessment

→ Students will draw pictures of how the character has changed. The drawings will be labeled with details from the text. Students will write or dictate corresponding sentences describing the character's change.

Text Selection

→ "The Boy Who Loved Books"

→ Text is a story written in paragraph form.

Materials

→ *The Boy Who Loved Books* passage, one copy per student (page 92; boywholovedbooks.pdf)

→ *Slowly Changing* activity (page 93)

→ *Hector Forever* activity (page 94)

→ *Hector Forever Reflection Page* (page 95)

Text-Dependent Questions (See pages 43–45 for more information.)

→ What is this text about?

→ If you had to use one word from the text to describe what this story is about, what word would you use?

→ How can we use the context to figure out the meanings of unfamiliar words?

→ How does Hector change? What words or descriptions help us understand how he changes?

→ Could this story really happen? Why? Why not?

The Boy Who Loved Books (cont.)

Areas of Complexity

	Measure	Explanation
Quantitative	Lexile Level	400L
Qualitative	Meaning or Purpose	This literary passage relates a story about a boy and what he loves. Imagery and word play are used to describe a character as he transforms. Students must interpret details to understand that the boy has physically become a book at the end.
	Structure	The passage is a narrative with a sequence of events and details that provide description for the sequence of events.
	Language Features	Words that have multiple meanings are used in word play throughout the passage.
Reader/ Task	Knowledge Demands	Students must have familiarity with the physical properties of books. Students must use key details to understand that the character becomes a book to complete the performance task.

Text Synopsis

Hector loves books so much that one day, he starts to take on their characteristics. Over time, Hector's skin becomes like leather and his spine stiffens as he eventually becomes a book on a shelf. But don't worry. Hector loves books so much, he is happy about it!

Differentiation

Additional Support—Provide a language experience mini-lesson with students who need additional support. Bring a leather-covered book, and allow students to use their senses to describe it. Provide necessary vocabulary to help students describe the book in order for them to adequately understand "The Boy Who Loved Books."

Extension—Have students think of something they love. Students can write or draw about how they would change into that object.

Phase 1—Hitting the Surface

Who Reads	Annotations (See page 58.)		
☑ teacher	☐ highlight main points	☐ underline key details	☑ write questions
☐ students	☑ circle key vocabulary	☐ arrows for connections	☐ other: _____

Procedure

1. Tell students that they will listen to and read a story several times. Each time will be for a different purpose, to gain a better understanding of the story.

2. Display a copy of "The Boy Who Loved Books" (page 92). Have students follow along as you read the passage aloud. Their goal is to get an overall idea of the story.

3. Ask students, "What is this passage about?"

4. After a brief discussion, ask students to follow along and try to understand more about the story as you read the text aloud.

5. **Partners**—After students have listened to you read the story, ask partners to briefly retell key details.

6. **Whole Class**—Regroup as a class, and display the text for all students. Ask students to share their responses to the initial question. Make annotations on your copy of the text.

7. If needed, ask additional layered/scaffolded questions, such as:
   - Who is the character in this story?
   - What is the setting?
   - How does Hector feel about books? How do you know?
   - How does Hector change during the text?
   - What happens at the end?

8. Have students share any words that are challenging. Guide them to clarify the words throughout future readings.

Phase 2—Digging Deeper

Who Reads	Annotations (See page 58.)		
☑ teacher	☑ highlight main points	☑ underline key details	☐ write questions
☐ students	☐ circle key vocabulary	☑ arrows for connections	☐ other: _____

The Boy Who Loved Books *(cont.)*

Phase 2—Digging Deeper *(cont.)*

Procedure

1. Review the story by asking students, "If you had to use one word to describe what this story is about, what word would you use?" If needed, guide students to notice how often books are mentioned in the story through the following scaffolded activity.

   • Read the text aloud as students follow along.

   • Ask students to listen for details related to the main idea, books. Each time you read about a concept related to books (shelves, pages, etc.), have students hold their palms together in front of them as if forming books.

   • Have a student scribe annotate the displayed copy of the text by highlighting a detail word each time the class holds up their "books."

2. Take a closer look at some of the unknown vocabulary words that are circled on the text. Point out where those circled words are in relation to the highlighted sentences. Have students listen to answer the question *How can we use context to figure out the meaning of this word?*

3. If necessary (or if students are new to close reading), you may need to model using context clues for unfamiliar words. Underline details (text or image) that help define the words, and write short definitions or draw pictures to represent the words in the margin on the projected copy for everyone to see.

   • For example: "I do not know the word *Hobbit*. I see that it is capitalized like it is the name of something. I also see that it is with the name *Harry Potter*. I also see in the previous sentence that the text is talking about a bookshelf. Since I know that *Harry Potter* is the name of a book, I think that *Hobbit* is also the name of a book." Reread the sentence to see if that makes sense in the context. Annotate the text by drawing arrows to show connections and underlining details that help you determine the meaning of words.

4. **Partners**—Have partners work together to use context clues to determine the meaning of the other circled words on the page. Support students in determining word meanings by asking additional layered/scaffolded questions about the text such as:

   • Does this word relate to books? Is it not related to books? How do you know?

   • What other words in the sentence do you understand?

   • What does the sentence before/after say that may help?

   • Does what you think the word means make sense in the sentence?

5. **Whole Class**—Regroup as a class, and display the text for all students. Ask students to share their responses to the vocabulary words. Have them support their responses with their annotations. Record student annotations on the displayed copy of the text.

Phase 3—Going Even Deeper

Who Reads

☑ teacher

☐ students

Annotations (See page 58.)

☐ highlight main points   ☑ underline key details   ☐ write questions

☐ circle key vocabulary   ☑ arrows for connections   ☐ other:_____

Procedure

1. Review with students that as they reread texts, they often learn new things about the text because of the different reasons for which it is read. Tell students that they will reread the text again to answer the questions *How does Hector change? What words or descriptions help us understand how he changes?*

2. Reread the first sentence of the second paragraph with students. Discuss what it means for good friends to look like each other. Tell students to continue to look for how Hector changes and how we know he changes as they continue to read.

3. Read the second sentence in the second paragraph. Annotate the text by drawing arrows to show the connection between Hector's body parts and what is happening to him. For example, draw an arrow from the word *spine* to the word *stiffen* in the second paragraph.

4. As you continue to read, have students annotate the text by drawing arrows to show connections between Hector and how he is changing in order to answer the initial questions. This can be done under your guidance on the displayed copy or by student pairs on individual copies depending on the needs of your students. Alternatively, students can draw the stages of Hector's change in the margins.

5. Provide students with the *Slowly Changing* activity (page 93). Have them complete the chart using the annotations they have made.

6. **Whole Class**—Regroup as a class, and review students' annotations of the text and *Slowly Changing* activity.

7. Conclude this phase by asking the questions *What is the meaning of this story?* and *What is the author telling us through this story?* Have students provide textual evidence for their reasoning as you discuss the questions.

Performance Assessment

1. Assign the performance task *Hector Forever* (page 94).

2. Guide students to think about their work and complete the *Hector Forever Reflection Page* (page 95).

The Boy Who Loved Books

1   Hector Quarto loved books. He looooved books. He L–O–V–E–D them. If you saw Hector, you saw a book. He was never without one.

2   Have you ever noticed how very good friends start to look like each other? It was no surprise when Hector's spine began to stiffen. His skin took on a paper-ish quality. When asked a question, Hector's mind riffled through his thoughts like the pages of a book.

3   Hector was becoming quite bookish.

4   As the years went by, his skin became leathery like the old books on the library shelves. In fact, Hector spent a lot of time there in the library. He just sat and stared at the shelves. He longed to be with the books he loved.

5   Hector's body got straighter. And stiffer. And then, very still.

6   Until one day, as Hector sat in the library, a tall man slowly wheeled a cart by him. The librarian reached out and grabbed Hector as though he weighed nothing and placed him on the bookshelf. Hector was thrilled to be on the shelf with his very good pals—the books. Hector looked up with glee and saw his reflection in the library window. But Hector's face wasn't reflected back. He saw just the image of books in a row, waiting to be chosen and read. Hector shook his head in wonder and saw one of the books on the shelf wiggle just a bit.

7   Hector closed his eyes and sighed a happy sigh. He would live forever with his books.

8   Forever and ever.

Slowly Changing

Directions: Tell how Hector changed. Copy words from the story for each body part.

Hector's Body Parts	How They Changed
spine	
skin	
hair	
round edges	
mind	
skin	
body	

Hector Forever

Directions: Draw a picture of Hector. Use words from the story to label the picture. Write a sentence to describe Hector.

Hector Forever Reflection Page

Directions: Think about your work. Did you follow directions?
Circle the *thumbs up* or *thumbs down* picture for each part.

What I Think about My Work

	Yes	No
My drawing has details.	👍	👎
I used words from the story.	👍	👎
My sentence describes Hector.	👍	👎

Teacher comments: _____

_____

_____

_____

_____

Rubric based on work by Lapp, D., B. Moss, M. Grant, & K. Johnson (2015)

It's About Time

Purpose

WHAT: Retell the story with events in the correct sequence.

HOW: Write a letter explaining what happened to a character.

I CAN: I can tell what happened in a story.

Standards

➔ **Reading:** Answer questions about key details in a text.

➔ **Writing:** Write to explain a series of events.

➔ **Language:** Make real-life connections between words and their use.

Performance Assessment

➔ Students will write letters to "the guys" to explain why he is too tired to play in the baseball game.

Text Selection

➔ "It's About Time"

➔ Text is organized in paragraphs in sequential order.

Materials

➔ *It's About Time* passage, one copy per student (page 102; itsabouttime.pdf)

➔ *Delays, Delays* activity (page 103)

➔ *I'm Too Tired* activity (page 104)

➔ *I'm Too Tired Reflection Page* (page 105)

Text-Dependent Questions (See pages 46–48 for more information.)

➔ What is the story about?

➔ What delays does the character face?

➔ What is the order of the delays?

➔ How does the character respond to each delay?

It's About Time (cont.)

Areas of Complexity

	Measure	Explanation
Quantitative	Lexile Level	500L
Qualitative	Meaning or Purpose	The text describes the delays that a boy encounters as he tries to get to the park to play with friends. Details are stated explicitly, but the overall affect to the character builds more subtly.
	Structure	The passage is in sequential order. Time elements are added throughout to show the delays the character encounters.
	Language Features	Everyday language is used to describe the basic sequence of events. Some precise vocabulary is used as added description, but is not necessary to understanding the sequence of events.
Reader/ Task	Knowledge Demands	Students must understand the unusual nature of the number of delays faced by the character to fully enjoy the humor of the story. Students must understand the sequence of details in the story to complete the performance task.

Text Synopsis

The main character needs to get to the park to meet the guys for the championship baseball game, but along the way, delay after delay eat away at the time he has to get there. Will he make it on time? Read to find out.

Differentiation

Additional Support—Write the time delays that are listed in paragraph 6 in the margins of the text. Provide students with instructional clocks as you read the story. Have students move the instructional clocks as you read aloud the text so they can see the time passing by.

Extension—Have students write about one more delay that could happen to make the character late for the baseball game.

Phase 1—Hitting the Surface

Who Reads
- ☐ teacher
- ☑ students

Annotations (See page 59.)
- ☑ highlight main points
- ☑ underline key details
- ☐ write questions
- ☐ circle key vocabulary
- ☐ arrows for connections
- ☐ other: _____

Procedure

1. Tell students that they will read a story several times. Each time will be for a different purpose, to gain a better understanding of the story.

2. Have students read and annotate the passage to get an overall idea of the story to answer the question *What is this story about?*

3. After students have read and annotated the text once, let them know you will read the text aloud. As you read the text, have students follow along and mark the main idea and key details.

4. **Partners**—After students have listened to you read the story, ask partners to briefly retell the story.

5. If needed, ask additional layered/scaffolded questions, such as:
   - Who is the character?
   - What is the setting? Does the setting change?
   - What is the problem(s)? What is wrong?
   - What is the solution? How does the problem get solved?

6. **Whole Class**—Regroup as a class, and display "It's About Time" (page 102) for all students. Ask students to share their responses to the question regarding what the story is about. Have them support their responses with their annotations. If possible, record student annotations on a displayed copy of the text.

7. Students should also bring any challenging words to your attention. Guide students to use context clues to clarify key words throughout future readings.

It's About Time *(cont.)*

Phase 2—Digging Deeper

Who Reads	Annotations (See page 59.)		
☐ teacher	☐ highlight main points	☑ underline key details	☐ write questions
☑ students	☐ circle key vocabulary	☐ arrows for connections	☑ other: <u>write numbers in the paragraph margins</u>

Procedure

1. Review the story elements from Phase 1 of the lesson. Explain to students that they will dig deeper into the text to identify the sequence of the delays. By understanding the sequence, they will be able to better retell the story.

2. Have students reread the text to identify the sequence of delays that the character encounters. Students should read to answer the questions *What delays does the character face?* and *What is the order of the delays?* Ask students to annotate the text by writing numbers in the margins to show the order in which the delays take place. Students can also underline key details in each paragraph to show which delay is described in the paragraph.

3. **Partners**—After students have read and annotated the text, pairs can share their thinking as related to the sequence of events.

4. **Whole Class**—Regroup as a class, and display the text for all students. Ask students to share their responses to the question regarding the sequence of the delays. Have them support their responses with their annotations. If possible, record student annotations on a displayed copy of the text.

5. Provide students with copies of the *Delays, Delays* activity (page 103). Have them complete this activity by describing each delay the character faces in the story.

6. **Partners**—After students complete the activity, have pairs practice retelling the story using the *Delays, Delays* activity as needed to remind them of the sequence and details of the delays in the story.

7. Display a clean copy of the text so students can see it. Reread the text with students. Ask students to point one hand's index finger at the other hand's wrist as if pointing to a watch every time they hear a reference to time as you read. Annotate the text by highlighting each reference.

8. Discuss the title of the passage. If needed, ask students layered/scaffolded questions to help them understand the title, such as:
   - What does it mean when someone says, "It's about time?"
   - How is time used throughout the passage? How is time related to the end of the passage?
   - What does the title have to do with the sequence of events/delays in the text?

Phase 3—Going Even Deeper

Who Reads

☐ teacher

☑ students

Annotations (See page 59.)

☐ highlight main points ☑ underline key details ☐ write questions

☑ circle key vocabulary ☑ arrows for connections ☐ other: _____

Procedure

1. Review with students that there is a character who is experiencing all the delays in the story. Tell students that as they reread the text, they will focus on the character to answer the question *How does the character respond to each delay?*

2. Have students reread the text to answer the question *How does the character respond to each delay?* Ask students to annotate the text by underlining key details that show the delay, circling key vocabulary that shows his response, and then draw arrows to show connections to the delay he encounters when he makes that response.

3. If needed, model with paragraph three. Say, "I see the problem the character faces is a flat tire. I'm going to underline the key detail *flat tire*. I also notice that the character's first reaction is *No!* After he figures out he can walk instead of ride his bike, his response is *I've got this!* I'm going to circle those words that show his response and draw an arrow from the words back to the flat tire. By reading this, I see that he is initially frustrated and mad about the flat tire, but then he figures out another way of getting to the game, and he figures he has it under control by responding, *I've got this!*"

4. **Partners**—After students have read and annotated the text once, pairs can share their thinking as related to the question about the character's response.

5. **Whole Class**—Regroup as a class, and display the text for all students. Ask students to share their ideas regarding the character's responses. Have them support their responses with their annotations. If possible, record student annotations on a displayed copy of the text.

Performance Assessment

1. Assign the performance task *I'm Too Tired* (page 104).

2. Guide students to think about their work and complete the *I'm Too Tired Reflection Page* (page 105).

It's About Time

1   The guys ask me to meet them at 2:00 in the park for our championship baseball game. My swimming lesson at the gym is done at 12:45. It takes 10 minutes to bike to the park from the gym. That's plenty of time, I think.

2   Think again.

3   A little kid in the class before mine won't get out of the pool. The lifeguard has to chase him for 10 minutes and then carry him out! So, my class starts late and ends just before 1:00. Still plenty of time though, right? Nope.

4   I rush outside and grab my bike. No! I've got a flat tire! But I can walk there in 30 minutes. I've got this!

5   But then halfway there, I hit a roadblock. Seriously? A fire hydrant burst, and water is gushing everywhere! Everyone has to turn around. I go back to the gym and take another route. I'm starting to wonder if I'll ever make it to the game.

6   I walk past Mr. Ketschum's house, the cranky man who lives on the corner. I'm watching for him and don't notice his trash can on the curb. Whammo! I knock it over, so of course he makes me clean it up. Tick, tock. Tick, tock.

7   Five minutes later, I finish the job and start to jog to the park. I do the math in my head. First, I had seventy-five minutes. Ten minutes went to the late lesson. Thirty minutes went to the detour and back. Five minutes went to the trash pickup, and thirty minutes went to walking and then jogging the new route.

8   I finally make it to the game and wave to the guys. The game is about to start. The only problem is now I'm too tired to play!

Delays, Delays

Directions: Write about each delay in the story. Use details from the story.

Swimming Pool Delay

_____

_____

Bike Delay

_____

_____

Roadblock Delay

_____

_____

Mr. Ketschum's House Delay

_____

_____

I'm Too Tired

Directions: Write a letter to the guys. Tell them about the delays on the way to the park. Write about the delays in order. Ask the guys to play the game tomorrow.

Dear _____,

_____

_____

_____

_____

_____

_____

Sincerely,

_____

I'm Too Tired Reflection Page

Directions: Think about your work. Write a check mark in the *Yes* or *No* column to show if you did all parts of the project.

What I Think about My Work

	Yes	No
I explained what happened on the way to the park.		
I wrote about the delays in order.		
I asked the guys to play the game tomorrow.		

Teacher comments: _____

_____

_____

_____

_____

Rubric based on work by Lapp, D., B. Moss, M. Grant, & K. Johnson (2015)

Bobbing Daisies

Purpose

WHAT: Comprehend story elements presented in a poem.

HOW: Illustrate and describe the events in a poem.

I CAN: I can show what happened in a poem.

Standards

→ **Reading:** With guidance and support, recognize common types of text.

→ **Writing:** With guidance and support, write/dictate ideas related to a text.

→ **Language:** With guidance and support, determine new meanings for familiar words.

Performance Assessment

→ Students will illustrate and use new words to describe what the character dreams about in the poem.

Text Selection

→ "Bobbing Daisies"

→ Text is a rhyming poem written in two stanzas.

Materials

→ *Bobbing Daisies* passage, one copy per student (page 112; bobbingdaisies.pdf)

→ *What Are They Doing?* activity (page 113)

→ *Dreaming* activity (page 114)

→ *Dreaming Reflection Page* (page 115)

Text-Dependent Questions (See pages 40–42 for more information.)

→ What is the text about?

→ What is special about the way the text is written?

→ What happens in the text?

→ Who are the characters?

→ What is the setting?

→ What words do you need to understand better? How can you learn more about the words?

→ What is happening in each stanza?

Bobbing Daisies (cont.)

Areas of Complexity

	Measure	Explanation
Quantitative	Lexile Level	Non-prose
Qualitative	Meaning or Purpose	This poem describes a child's love for how daisies look in a field and how she will dream of them when she goes to bed.
	Structure	The text is a poem written in two four-lined stanzas. The second and fourth line of each stanza rhyme.
	Language Features	This is a rhyming poem. The flowers are personified. The narrator is unnamed and not described.
Reader/ Task	Knowledge Demands	Students must understand the setting switch that takes place between stanzas from a field of daisies to a child dreaming about the daisies. Students must comprehend the story elements and understand new words to complete the performance assessment.

Text Synopsis

This short poem describes a field of daisies bobbing in the sun. The narrator says good night to the daisies and then dreams of them.

Differentiation

Additional Support—Bring in photographs of a single daisy or a real daisy if possible. Discuss the various parts of the daisy, including why the round part might be described as a head. Have students draw and label a picture of a daisy with the stem, center, and petals.

Extension—Have students write about something they love and dream about. Encourage them to write in the format of a poem.

Bobbing Daisies *(cont.)*

Phase 1—Hitting the Surface

Who Reads	Annotations (See page 58.)		
☑ teacher	☐ highlight main points	☐ underline key details	☐ write questions
☐ students	☑ circle key vocabulary	☑ arrows for connections	☐ other: _____

Procedure

1. Tell students that they will listen to a poem several times. Each time will be for a different purpose, to gain a better understanding of the poem.

2. Display a copy of "Bobbing Daisies" (page 112). Have students listen as you read the passage to get an overall idea of the poem.

3. Ask students, "What is this text about?"

4. **Partners**—After students have listened to you read the poem once, ask partners to briefly retell key details.

5. **Whole Class**—Regroup as a class, and display the text for all students. Ask students to share their responses to the initial question. Make annotations on your copy of the text.

Bobbing Daisies (cont.)

Phase 2—Digging Deeper

Who Reads | Annotations (See page 58.)

☑ teacher   ☑ highlight main points   ☑ underline key details   ☐ write questions

☐ students   ☑ circle key vocabulary   ☐ arrows for connections   ☑ other: <u>pronouns to show character</u>

Procedure

1. Remind students that each time they read a text, they learn a little more about it. This time they will listen to how the text is written.

2. Display and read the poem aloud again. Ask students, "What is special about the way the text is written?"

3. If needed, ask additional layered/scaffolded questions such as:
   - Is it longer, shorter, or the same length as other stories you know?
   - What is special about the way the words sound?
   - What is the mood? Does it feel silly, serious, sad, or something else?

4. As you read it again, ask students to try to understand what is happening in the poem.

5. Ask students, "What happens in the text?"

6. If needed, ask additional layered/scaffolded questions such as:
   - Who are the characters?
   - Who is talking in the poem?
   - What is the setting?
   - Where are the daisies bobbing in the daytime?
   - Where are the daisies bobbing at night?

7. Partners—Have students work together to answer the 5Ws for the poem. Who? What? When? Where? Why?

8. If students are having difficulty identifying the two settings, provide them with sheets of paper that have been folded in half. Have students draw the setting from the first stanza on one half of the paper and the setting from the second stanza on the second half. Reread the poem so students have a better and more distinct representation of each setting while listening to each stanza.

Bobbing Daisies (cont.)

Phase 3—Going Even Deeper

Who Reads	Annotations (See page 58.)		
☑ teacher	☐ highlight main points	☐ underline key details	☑ write questions
☐ students	☑ circle key vocabulary	☐ arrows for connections	☐ other: _____

Procedure

1. Explain that students will listen to the poem again. This time, they will listen for specific words that help them understand what the characters are doing in the poem.

2. Display the poem for students to see. Let the students know you will work together to circle all of the words you would like to better understand.

3. Read the first line of the poem and ask, "Is there a word you would like to better understand?"

4. Guide a student to circle any unfamiliar words on the displayed text.

5. Have students think about the question *How can you better understand the circled words?* Model or guide students to use nearby words to understand the unfamiliar words.

6. **Partners**—Have students work together to discuss the phrase *tucking in their heads.* Pairs can share their thinking as related to the initial question. Support students by asking layered/scaffolded questions, such as:
   - What part of a daisy would be the head?
   - How would a daisy get tucked in?
   - How does the word *gently* help you better understand the movement?

7. **Whole Class**—Regroup as a class, and display the text for all students. Ask students to share their responses to the question regarding the phrase *tucking in their heads.*

8. Tell students that they will use their knowledge of the characters and setting as well as the vocabulary words that were discussed to show what the daisies are doing and what the narrator is doing in the poem. Provide students with the *What Are They Doing?* activity (page 113). Have students draw pictures of what the poem says the daisies are doing and what the character is doing.

Performance Assessment

1. Assign the performance task *Dreaming* (page 114).

2. Guide students to think about their work and complete the *Dreaming Reflection Page* (page 115).

Bobbing Daisies

1   I love a field of daisies
    Bobbing in the sun,
    Gently tucking in their heads
    When the day is done.

2   I say, "Good night, daisies!"
    And "Good night, sun!"
    Then bob with daisies in my dreams
    When the day is done.

What Are They Doing?

Directions: Draw what the daisies do in part 1. Draw what the narrator does in part 2.

Part 1—Daisies

Part 2—Narrator

Dreaming

Directions: Draw a picture of the narrator's dream. Write a sentence about the dream. Use words you learned.

_____

- -

_____

Note: Students may dictate their sentence to the teacher.

Dreaming Reflection Page

Directions: Think about your work. Did you follow directions? Circle the *thumbs up* or *thumbs down* picture for each part.

What I Think about My Work

	Yes	No
My drawing clearly shows what the narrator is dreaming about.	👍	👎
My sentence matches my drawing.	👍	👎
My sentence uses a word I learned during this lesson.	👍	👎

Teacher comments: _____

_____

_____

_____

_____

_____

Rubric based on work by Lapp, D., B. Moss, M. Grant, & K. Johnson (2015)

51540—Dive into Close Reading

Around the World in Forty Winks

Purpose

WHAT: Understand the *where* and *when* of the setting.

HOW: Draw and write the *where* and *when* of the setting.

I CAN: I can describe the setting of a story.

Standards

→ **Reading:** Identify words that appeal to the senses.

→ **Writing:** Draw and write in response to a prompt.

→ **Language:** Determine the meaning of words or phrases.

Performance Assessment

→ Students will draw and write about another place in the world the boy from the story could travel. They will also describe how he will get there.

Text Selection

→ "Around the World in Forty Winks"

→ Text is written in paragraph form. Some dialog is included.

Materials

→ *Around the World in Forty Winks* passage, one copy per student (page 122; fortywinks.pdf)

→ *Places Around the World* activity (page 123)

→ *Tomorrow Night* activity (page 124)

→ *Tomorrow Night Reflection Page* (page 125)

Text-Dependent Questions (See pages 43–45 for more information.)

→ What is this story about?

→ When does the story take place?

→ How do the words the author chose help you understand when the story happens?

→ What words help you understand the places the boy goes?

→ What words did the author choose to describe how the boy travels?

Around the World in Forty Winks *(cont.)*

Areas of Complexity

	Measure	Explanation
Quantitative	Lexile Level	390L
Qualitative	Meaning or Purpose	This text tells the story of a little boy and his dream. All of the events actually take place in a dream.
	Structure	This text begins with a typical sequence of events but then switches to a dream.
	Language Features	Precise and sophisticated vocabulary is used throughout the story
Reader/ Task	Knowledge Demands	The text references landmarks with which students may not be familiar. Students must recognize and add to the pattern of the story to complete the performance task.

Text Synopsis

It is bedtime for a little boy and his dog. But once his eyes close, he takes off on a trip around the world in his dream. He flies to see landmarks such as the Eiffel Tower, Big Ben, and Loch Ness. He heads for home as the sun begins to rise, but he knows he will fly somewhere else tomorrow.

Differentiation

Additional Support—Provide visual support for the landmarks the boy flies to in his dream. Download images of the Eiffel Tower, Big Ben, and Loch Ness so students have a more concrete understanding of what they are. Relate them to another landmark students may be familiar with such as the Statue of Liberty. You may also wish to point out their locations on a map and discuss with students how long it would take to get to each one. Ask if the boy in the text would be able to get to these locations in one night.

Extension—Students will study more about word choices the author uses instead of the word *fly*. Have students choose another verb. Make a list of words that show the nuances when used. For example, students could use the word *walk* or *see*.

Phase 1—Hitting the Surface

Who Reads	Annotations (See page 58.)		
☑ teacher	☐ highlight main points	☑ underline key details	☑ write questions
☐ students	☑ circle key vocabulary	☐ arrows for connections	☐ other: _____

Procedure

1. Tell students that they will listen to and read a story several times. Each time will be for a different purpose, to gain a better understanding of the story.

2. Display a copy of "Around the World in Forty Winks" (page 122). Have students follow along as you read the passage aloud. Their goal is to get an overall idea of the story.

3. Ask students, "What is this passage about?"

4. After brief discussion, ask students to follow along and try to understand more about the story as you read the text aloud.

5. **Partners**—After students have listened to you read the story, ask partners to briefly retell key details.

6. **Whole Class**—Regroup as a class, and display the text for all students. Ask students to share their responses to the initial question. Make annotations on your copy of the text.

7. If needed, ask additional layered/scaffolded questions, such as:
   - Who are the characters in the story?
   - What is the setting? What does the illustration show about the setting? Is there more than one setting?
   - What events happen in the story?
   - Could these events happen in real life?
   - Who is Explorer?
   - What are the settings?
   - Does the mom go with the boy and dog? How do you know?

8. Have students share any words that are challenging. Guide them to clarify the words throughout future readings.

Phase 2—Digging Deeper

Who Reads	Annotations (See page 58.)		
☐ teacher	☐ highlight main points	☑ underline key details	☐ write questions
☑ students	☐ circle key vocabulary	☐ arrows for connections	☐ other: _____

Phase 2—Digging Deeper *(cont.)*

Procedure

1. Explain that during this reading, they will take a closer look at how the author chose words and how the illustrator designed the pictures to craft the settings. Review with students that the setting is the time and place of the story.

2. Display the text for students to see. Tell students to listen for the answers to the question *When does this story take place?* Read the first sentence aloud. Ask students to underline a single word that describes the setting.

3. **Partners**—Have partners work together to reread the last three paragraphs of the text and annotate for ways in which the author described the time setting: *tonight*. If students are not yet fluent readers, have them talk about the three paragraphs you have just read. If needed, ask additional layered/scaffold questions to partners, such as:

   - How does each word or phrase that you annotate relate to the word *tonight*? For example, "I see that the mom says, 'See you in the morning.' and that she turns out the light. This shows me that it is bedtime for the little boy."
   - What other words refer to night?
   - What other activities happen at night?
   - How do you know the *night* is over?

4. **Whole Class**—Regroup as a class, and display the text for all students to see. Ask students to share their responses regarding the time setting: *tonight*. Ask, "How do the words the author chose help you understand *when* the story happens?"

5. Then, ask the question: *What evidence is there in the illustration to support the setting: tonight?* After they have had time to view the illustration, discuss with them evidence they see in the illustrations.

6. Remind students that the setting is also *where* the story takes place. Explain that the boy goes to some famous places in the world. Tell students you will reread the second and fourth paragraphs. They should listen closely to answer the question *What words help you understand where the boy goes?*

7. Provide students with the *Places Around the World* activity (page 123), and have them complete the activity with partners or individually. Students may not know the names of places, such as the Eiffel Tower, but should be able to use the text to help them find out more about these famous places. Reread sections of the text as needed, and ask layered/scaffolded questions such as:

   - What clue do we have about what kind of structure the Eiffel Tower is in the name? Does the illustration give clues about what the Eiffel Tower is?
   - What clues do we have about what kind of structure Big Ben is? Does the illustration give clues about what Big Ben is? What word is used to describe how Big Ben sounds?

8. **Whole Class**—Review students' responses to the *Places Around the World* activity. Ask students, "If the little boy closes his eyes at night/bedtime and then travels to places all over the world, what does this mean?"

Phase 3—Going Even Deeper

Who Reads

☐ teacher

☑ students

Annotations (See page 58.)

☐ highlight main points   ☐ underline key details   ☐ write questions

☑ circle key vocabulary   ☐ arrows for connections   ☐ other:_____

Procedure

1. Display a copy of the text for students to see. Review the title of the passage with students. Tell students that the purpose of rereading the text this time is to answer the question *What words did the author choose?*

2. Read aloud the last sentence of the text. Circle the word *fly*. Explain that the author could have used the word *fly* over and over again throughout the text; however, he uses other words that help us understand that the boy flew all around. Reread the first four paragraphs. Ask students to define or describe the word *fly*. After someone defines it, invite them to act it out.

3. Circle the word *soaring* in the last sentence of the fourth paragraph. Have students act out this word. Define and model as needed.

4. Have students reread the fifth paragraph with you to identify other words the author uses to describe how the boy gets around. Students can annotate their text by circling the words they see or hear.

5. **Partners**—After students have read and annotated the text, pairs can share their thinking as related to the question about the author's word choice.

6. **Whole Class**—Regroup as a class, and display the text for all students. Ask students to share their responses to the question about word choice. Record student annotations on a displayed copy of the text.

7. Create a list of the words the author uses for *flying*: *soaring*, *sailed*, *zoomed*, and *skimmed*. Work with students to act out these words so they understand the nuances between each word and its use. Ask *How did the author's use of these words enhance the text rather than repeating the word* fly *over and over throughout the text?*

8. Reread the text one last time. When finished, ask students if the boy and his dog were really flying? What was the author trying to tell us?

Performance Assessment

1. Assign the performance task *Tomorrow Night* (page 124). Provide a sentence frame as needed, such as: The boy will _____ to _____.

2. Guide students to think about their work and complete the *Tomorrow Night Reflection Page* (page 125).

Around the World in Forty Winks

1 "Where to tonight?" my mom said.

2 "I want to go to France," I said. "Or maybe England!"

3 "See you in the morning, my little man," she called as she turned out the light.

4 I buried myself under my blanket and pulled my dog, Explorer, closer. Together, we closed our eyes. Soon, we were soaring.

5 We sailed over the Eiffel Tower. It lit up the sky with golden lights. We zoomed past Big Ben in London and heard it chime. Then, we turned north and skimmed over Loch Ness in Scotland. Explorer waved to Nessie who gave a friendly "monster" wink before diving beneath the water.

6 In the distance, we could see the sun rising. It was time to come home. Side by side, we flew. Tomorrow we would fly again.

Places Around the World

Directions: Use the story to tell about these places. Draw or write your answers.

Name— What is it?			
Place— Where is it?			
More— What is special?			

Tomorrow Night

Directions: Draw a picture of where the boy and Explorer will go next. Write a sentence about what they will see.

_____

- -

_____

- -

_____

Tomorrow Night Reflection Page

Directions: Think about your work. Did you follow directions? Circle the *thumbs up* or *thumbs down* picture for each part.

What I Think about My Work

	Yes	No
My drawing clearly shows where the boy and Explorer will go.	👍	👎
My sentence matches my drawing.	👍	👎
My sentence describes how the boy and Explorer will see.	👍	👎

Teacher comments: _____

_____

_____

_____

_____

Rubric based on work by Lapp, D., B. Moss, M. Grant, & K. Johnson (2015)

Love Like Salt

Purpose

WHAT: Identify a character's point of view.

HOW: Write descriptions of story events from one character's point of view.

I CAN: I can describe a story from a character's point of view.

Standards

→ **Reading:** Read to identify point of view.

→ **Writing:** Write a description of fictional events.

→ **Language:** Identify and use adjectives and adverbs.

Performance Assessment

→ Students will describe events from the story from the king's point of view.

Text Selection

→ "Love Like Salt"

→ Text is a story told in paragraph form. The story is in sequential form and contains dialog.

Materials

→ *Love Like Salt* passage, one copy per student (page 132; lovelikesalt.pdf)

→ *Character Adjective Sort* activity (page 133)

→ *Thinking Like the King* activity (page 134)

→ *Thinking Like the King Reflection Page* (page 135)

Text-Dependent Questions (See pages 46–48 for more information.)

→ What is this text about?

→ What is the point of view of the king? How do you know?

→ What is the point of view of the third daughter? What words tell you this?

→ How can I use my voice to show the character's point of view as I read aloud the text?

Love Like Salt (cont.)

Areas of Complexity

	Measure	Explanation
Quantitative	Lexile Level	600L
Qualitative	Meaning or Purpose	The text tells a story of a king who learns a lesson.
	Structure	The story is written in sequential paragraph form. There is dialog between the characters.
	Language Features	Commonly used language describes the basic sequence of events. Some precise vocabulary is used as added description but is not necessary to understanding the sequence of events.
Reader/ Task	Knowledge Demands	Students must have some basic understanding of similes. Students must know that salt adds flavor when cooking. Students must understand and evaluate characters to complete the performance assessment.

Text Synopsis

A king returns from a trip and asks his daughters if they are glad to see him. One daughter tells him that his return is *as good as salt*. The king does not understand and banishes her from the castle. She sneaks back a few weeks later and convinces the cook to keep the salt out of food. When the king realizes that the food is bland, the princess reveals herself and explains why. The king realizes the intent of her original comment about salt. He sees what a fool he has been and welcomes her home.

Differentiation

Additional Support—Identify and discuss other similes so students can better understand how the comparison works. For example:

- black as night
- gentle as a lamb
- soft as silk
- wise as an owl
- white as snow
- busy as a bee

Extension—Have students write similes for how they would describe a king's return after a long journey.

Phase 1—Hitting the Surface

Who Reads	Annotations (See page 59.)		
☐ teacher	☑ highlight main points	☐ underline key details	☐ write questions
☑ students	☑ circle key vocabulary	☐ arrows for connections	☐ other: _____

Procedure

1. Tell students that they will read a story several times. Each time will be for a different purpose, to gain a better understanding of the story.

2. Have students read and annotate the passage to get an overall idea of the story to answer the question *What is this story about?*

3. After students have read and annotated the text once, let them know you will read the text aloud. Have students follow along as you read the text and mark the main idea and key details.

4. **Partners**—After students have listened to you read the story, ask partners to briefly retell the story and identify the main characters.

5. If needed, ask additional layered/scaffolded questions, such as:
   · Who are the characters?
   · What is the setting?
   · What happens in the beginning, middle, and end?
   · What is the problem?
   · What is the solution? How does the problem get solved?

6. **Whole Class**—Regroup as a class, and display "Love Like Salt" (page 132) for all students. Ask students to share their responses to the question regarding what the story is about. Have them support their responses with their annotations. If possible, record student annotations on a displayed copy of the text.

7. Students should also bring any challenging words to your attention. Guide students to use context clues to clarify key words throughout subsequent readings.

Literary
Craft and Structure

Love Like Salt *(cont.)*

Phase 2—Digging Deeper

Who Reads	Annotations (See page 59.)		
☐ teacher	☐ highlight main points	☐ underline key details	☐ write questions
☑ students	☑ circle key vocabulary	☐ arrows for connections	☐ other: _____

Procedure

1. Tell students that they will work further with the text "Love Like Salt" to identify point of view.

2. Tell students, "Point of view is the way a character sees something. There can be one point of view or many points of view in a text. The author gives us clues about his or her point of view by what he or she says and does. It is a good reader's job to use the clues to figure out the point of view of a character."

3. Review the main characters that students identified in Phase 1: the third daughter and the king. Tell students they will reread the text to answer the questions *What is the point of view of the king?* and *What is the point of view of the third daughter?*

4. Tell students that adjectives used to describe characters are often clues about their points of view. Have students reread the text and annotate it by circling key vocabulary to show adjectives that describe each character.

5. **Partners**—After students have read and annotated the text once, pairs can share their thinking as related to the point of view of each character. If needed, ask layered/scaffolded questions, such as:

   · What does the third daughter compare the king's return to?
   · Does the king understand what this means? How do you know? What does this tell about the king?
   · How does the third daughter prove what she meant by her comment?
   · Now does the king understand what it means? How do you know? What does this tell about the king?
   · How does the king respond to his daughter once he understands what she meant? What does this tell about the king?

6. **Whole Class**—Regroup as a class, and display the text for all students. Ask students to share their responses to the question regarding each character's point of view. Have them support their responses with their annotations. If possible, record student annotations on a displayed copy of the text.

7. Provide students with copies of the *Character Adjective Sort* activity (page 133). Have students sort adjectives used in the text to describe the king and the princess.

Phase 3—Going Even Deeper

Who Reads	Annotations (See page 59.)		
☐ teacher	☐ highlight main points	☐ underline key details	☐ write questions
☑ students	☐ circle key vocabulary	☐ arrows for connections	☑ other: <u>write K (king) or D (daughter) in margins to show speaker</u>

Procedure

1. Tell students they will use the points of view they identified in the previous reading as they reread the text for a new purpose. Review the point of view of the third daughter and the king at various points in the story.

2. Have students reread the text to identify which lines of dialog and paragraphs are best connected with the king and which are best connected with the daughter. Have students annotate the text by writing *K* for *king* and *D* for *daughter* in the margins of the text.

3. **Partners**—Have pairs of students discuss and compare the annotations they made.

4. Discuss various tones of voice that would be appropriate for each character and his/her point of view. Have students reread the text to answer the question *How can I use my voice to show the character's point of view as I read aloud the text?* Allow time for students to practice using different voices to indicate each character's point of view.

5. **Partners**—Have pairs of students work together to read aloud the text. Partners can either read the entire text independently, changing voices to show each character, or partners can practice reading the text together. Each partner can portray the voice and point of view of either the king or the daughter.

6. **Whole Class**—Regroup as a class, and allow time for individuals or partner groups to perform what they practiced for the whole group.

Performance Assessment

1. Assign the performance task *Thinking Like the King* (page 134).

2. Guide students to think about their work and complete the *Thinking Like the King Reflection Page* (page 135).

Love Like Salt

1 A king returned from a long journey, cranky and tired from his travels. He called for his three daughters and asked each if she was glad to see him.

2 "Your return is like the sun coming out after days of darkness!" said the first girl. The king smiled.

3 "It is as though I was blind and now I can see!" said the second girl. The king beamed.

4 "Your return is as good as salt," said the third girl. "I love you like food loves salt."

5 "What foolishness!" cried the king.

6 The king became angry, thinking his daughter was making a joke of him. He banished her from the castle. The princess went to the home of a nearby shepherd who cared for the king's sheep. The shepherd and his family kindly took her in, and she lived with them for weeks.

7 One day, the princess heard about a large feast at the castle. She snuck into the castle and convinced the old cook to keep salt out of the food. The princess, disguised as a servant, then served the king.

8 "What is wrong with this food?" shouted the king. "Its flavor is bland and boring."

9 The princess stood tall before the king and said, "On my order, the cook left out the salt. I know you do not care for it."

10 "And who are you?" asked the king, confused.

11 "I am the girl who loves her father like salt," replied the princess.

12 The king shouted with joy as he recognized his daughter. He saw what a fool he had been. "Will you forgive me?" he asked her.

13 "With all my heart," said she.

14 And the kingdom returned to happiness.

Character Adjective Sort

Directions: Some adjectives in the Word Bank describe the king. Some adjectives describe the third daughter. Copy the adjectives to the correct side of the chart.

Word Bank

tired	forgiving	foolish	disguised	sneaky	cranky
angry	banished	simple	convincing	tired	joyful

King	Third Daughter

Thinking Like the King

Directions: Explain each event from the king's point of view. The first one has been done for you.

1. "Your return is as good as salt," said the third girl.

   <u>My daughter is making a joke of me.</u>

   _____

   _____

   _____

2. The princess, disguised as a servant, then served the king a plate of food with no salt.

   _____

   _____

   _____

   _____

3. "I am the girl who loves her father like salt," replied the princess.

   _____

   _____

   _____

   _____

Thinking Like the King Reflection Page

Directions: Think about your work. Write a check mark in the *Yes* or *No* column to show if you did all of the parts of the project.

What I Think about My Work

	Yes	No
I wrote from the king's point of view.		
My answers match details about the king from the story.		
I used **I**, **my**, or **me** to sound like the king		
I wrote a conclusion sentence.		

Teacher comments: _____

_____

_____

_____

_____

Rubric based on work by Lapp, D., B. Moss, M. Grant, & K. Johnson (2015)

How Colors Make Us Feel and The Color Game

Purpose

WHAT: Combine information from two texts.

HOW: Use details from two texts to draw and write about a color.

I CAN: I can use information from two texts.

Standards

➜ **Reading:** With guidance and support, compare and contrast two texts on a similar topic.

➜ **Writing:** With guidance and support, draw, write, or dictate about examples from the text.

➜ **Language:** Explore nuances in word meanings.

Performance Assessment

➜ Students will integrate knowledge of both texts to draw an object and describe how the color of the object makes them feel.

Text Selection

➜ "How Colors Make Us Feel"

➜ "The Color Game"

➜ "How Colors Make Us Feel" is in paragraph form.

➜ "The Color Game" is written as dialog between two characters.

Materials

➜ *How Colors Make Us Feel* and *The Color Game* passages, one copy per student (page 142; colors.pdf)

➜ *White, Yellow, Blue* activity (page 143)

➜ *My Color* activity (page 144)

➜ *My Color Reflection Page* (page 145)

Text-Dependent Questions (See pages 40–42 for more information.)

➜ What is this text about?

➜ What does the text say about each color?

➜ What colors are named in both texts?

➜ What is the same about what these texts say about color? What is different?

How Colors Make Us Feel and The Color Game (cont.)

Areas of Complexity

	Measure	Explanation
Quantitative	Lexile Level	"How Colors Make Us Feel"—560L "The Color Game"—380L
Qualitative	Meaning or Purpose	"How Colors Make Us Feel" describes the effects various colors can have on our feelings. "The Color Game" relates the story of two children playing a game to name objects of various colors.
	Structure	"How Colors Make Us Feel" names a color and then describes it. "The Color Game" is mainly written in dialog between two characters.
	Language Features	"How Colors Make Us Feel" uses colors to describe feelings, which may be a new idea for young children. "The Color Game" tells a story mostly through dialog.
Reader/ Task	Knowledge Demands	Students must keep the details of two different texts in mind in order to compare and contrast information in them. Students must remember details from the texts to complete the performance assessment.

Text Synopsis

"How Colors Make Us Feel" describes how colors can make people feel different things.

In "The Color Game," Jill and Tom are out for a walk on a winter day. They play a game naming objects they see that are the colors white, yellow, and blue. They decide it is time to go home when Jill's lips turn blue.

Differentiation

Additional Support—Provide students with a visual representation of the colors. Students may use a box of crayons, slips of colored paper, or colored manipulatives to help them identify each color named in the texts.

Extension—Have students identify how various colors make them feel. Students can draw pictures or write simple sentences to answer the question posed at the end of "How Colors Make Us Feel." Provide a sentence frame as needed, such as: _____ (color) makes me feel _____.

Phase 1—Hitting the Surface

Who Reads	Annotations (See page 58.)

Who Reads

☑ teacher

☐ students

Annotations (See page 58.)

☑ highlight main points ☐ underline key details ☐ write questions

☑ circle key vocabulary ☐ arrows for connections ☐ other: _____

Procedure

1. Tell students that they will listen to two texts several times. Each time will be for a different purpose, to gain a better understanding of the story.

2. Display a copy of the "How Colors Make Us Feel" (page 142). Have students listen as you read the passage to get an overall idea of the text.

3. Ask students, "What is this text about?"

4. **Partners**—After students have listened to you read the text once, ask partners to briefly retell key details.

5. **Whole Class**—Regroup as a class, and display the text for all students. Ask students to share their responses to the initial question. Make annotations on your copy of the text.

6. Display a copy of "The Color Game" (page 142). Have students listen to you read the passage to get an overall idea of the story.

7. Ask students, "What is this story about?"

8. **Partners**—After students have listened to you read the story once, ask partners to briefly retell the story using the correct sequence of events.

9. **Whole Class**—Regroup as a class, and display the text for all students. Ask students to share their responses to the initial question. Make annotations on your copy of the text.

How Colors Make Us Feel and The Color Game *(cont.)*

Phase 2—Digging Deeper

Who Reads / **Annotations (See page 58.)**

☑ teacher   ❑ highlight main points   ☑ underline key details   ❑ write questions

❑ students   ❑ circle key vocabulary   ❑ arrows for connections   ❑ other: _____

Procedure

1. Tell students that they will listen to both texts again to learn more about each.

2. First, reread "How Colors Make Us Feel." Have students listen to answer the question *What does the text say about each color?*

3. **Small Groups**—After students have listened to the passage again, small groups or pairs can share their thinking related to the question.

4. Create a two-columned chart. Title the left side *Color.* Title the right side *How It Makes Us Feel.*

5. **Whole Class**—Regroup as a class, and display the text for all students. Ask students to share their responses to the question regarding what the text says about each color. Annotate the text with students' responses by underlining key details. Record student responses on the two-columned chart as well. Leave the chart displayed for future reference.

6. Next, reread "The Color Game" aloud. Have students listen to answer the question *What does the text say about each color?* Ask students to visualize the walk that Tom and Jill are taking and the objects they see as they play the color game.

7. Provide students with the *White, Yellow, Blue* activity (page 143). Have them work individually or with partners to draw the objects of each color Jill and Tom see as they walk. Support students as needed by rereading and/or annotating the text.

Phase 3—Going Even Deeper

Who Reads
- ☑ teacher
- ☑ students

Annotations (See page 58.)
- ☐ highlight main points
- ☑ underline key details
- ☐ write questions
- ☐ circle key vocabulary
- ☑ arrows for connections
- ☐ other: _____

Procedure

1. Tell students that they will listen to "How Colors Make Us Feel" and "The Color Game" again for another purpose. This time, they will compare and contrast the two texts. This means they will find things that are the same and things that are different about the two texts.

2. Reread both texts to students. Have them listen to answer the question *What colors are named in both texts?*

3. Guide students to draw arrows connecting the same color words across both texts on the displayed copy. For example, a student will draw an arrow between the word *yellow* in the first text and the word *yellow* in the second text.

4. Reread the sentences with arrows. Ask, "What is the same about what these texts say about color? What is different?"

5. Ask students which color from "The Color Game" is not in "How Colors Make Us Feel." Refer to the two-columned chart and the activity sheet if students need support in identifying the missing color.

6. **Partners**—Ask students to answer the question posed at the end of "How Colors Make Us Feel" using the missing color. "How does white make you feel?" Allow students to discuss their ideas with partners.

Performance Assessment

1. Assign the performance task *My Color* (page 144).

2. Guide students to think about their work and complete the *My Color Reflection Page* (page 145).

How Colors Make Us Feel

1 Do some colors make you happy?

2 Red is the color of fire. It wakes us up. Yellow, the color of the sun, makes us smile. Colors like blue and green help people rest. You may sleep better in a blue room than in a red one. Brown and green make us calm. They make us think of trees and plants. Some people like orange. That is because it makes them think of Halloween!

3 How do colors make you feel?

The Color Game

1 On a cold winter day, Tom and his sister Jill went for a walk.

2 "I want to play a game," said Tom.

3 "We can play White, Yellow, Blue," Jill said.

4 Tom named two white things he saw as they were walking. "I see snow and ice."

5 Jill picked two yellow things. "I see the sun. And...my boots are yellow!"

6 "I want to go again!" Jill pleaded. "I see a blue scarf on that snowman."

7 "What is your second one?" Tom asked.

8 "I don't know," Jill sighed.

9 "Well, you are so cold that your lips are blue!" Tom laughed. "That means it is time to go home!"

White, Yellow, Blue

Directions: What objects do Tom and Jill name? Draw the object for each color.

White

Yellow

Blue

My Color

Directions: Play a color game. Choose a color. Draw an object you see that is that color. Use what you learned to describe how the object will make you feel.

_____

_ _ _ _ _ _ _ _ _ _ _ _ _ _ _ _

My color is _____ .

My object:

_____   _____

_ _ _ _ _ _ _ _   _ _ _ _ _ _ _ _

_____ makes me feel _____ .

Note: Students may dictate their sentences to the teacher.

Name: _____ Date: _____

My Color Reflection Page

Directions: Think about your work. Did you follow directions? Circle the *thumbs up* or *thumbs down* picture for each part.

What I Think about My Work

	Yes	No
I chose a color.	👍	👎
I drew an object with the color I chose.	👍	👎
I described how the color makes me feel.	👍	👎

Teacher comments: _____

_____

_____

_____

_____

_____

_____

Rubric based on work by Lapp, D., B. Moss, M. Grant, & K. Johnson (2015)

Al's Choice

Purpose

WHAT: Use details about a character to predict his actions.

HOW: Write a sentence predicting what a character will do and list supporting details from the text.

I CAN: I can predict a character's action.

Standards

→ **Reading:** Use details in a story to describe its characters, setting, or events.

→ **Writing:** With guidance and support, use information from a provided source to answer a question.

→ **Language:** Use words and phrases to signal simple relationships.

Performance Assessment

→ Students will use details from the text to predict the character's final choice.

Text Selection

→ "Al's Choice"

→ The text is a narrative with a flashback that disrupts the sequence of events. A moral dilemma is posed at the end of the selection.

Materials

→ *Al's Choice* passage, one copy per student (page 152; alschoice.pdf)

→ *What Should He Do?* activity (page 153)

→ *What Will He Do?* activity (page 154)

→ *What Will He Do? Reflection Page* (page 155)

Text-Dependent Questions (See pages 43–45 for more information.)

→ What is the story about?

→ Who are the characters?

→ What choices does Al have to make?

→ What are the reasons for and against Al's choices?

→ What does "the right thing" mean?

→ Why does Al think, *But maybe that boy wanted to see the movie as badly as I did. Maybe he had worked just as hard to earn the money?* What do you learn about Al from this statement?

Al's Choice (cont.)

Areas of Complexity

	Measure	Explanation
Quantitative	Lexile Level	520L
Qualitative	Meaning or Purpose	The purpose of the text is to relate the sequence of events leading up to a moral dilemma at the end of the passage.
	Structure	The structure of the passage may be challenging for beginning readers. The plot is not in sequential order and there is some internal dialog by the main character throughout.
	Language Features	The passage contains vocabulary that is sophisticated and precise that may interfere with understanding of the overall plot.
Reader/ Task	Knowledge Demands	Reasons made in the text must be identified and used to evaluate the choices the main character and the reader make at the end of the passage.

Text Synopsis

Al is on his way to pay for a baseball trip when he realizes that a movie he has been wanting to see is playing. First, he must decide whether to use the money he and his mother have worked so hard to save on a ticket. But, when the wind blows a ticket to the movie right over to him, he encounters a new dilemma when he realizes it belongs to a nearby boy who has lost it. What will he do? What would you do?

Differentiation

Additional Support—Provide students with practice in identifying choices and reasons. Students who are struggling with identifying reasons may benefit from the use of examples from their daily lives or with choices of characters from familiar books.

Extension—Have students identify choices characters have to make in other texts. Ask them to find the reasons for and against the choices and offer predictions about which choices the characters will make.

Al's Choice *(cont.)*

Phase 1—Hitting the Surface

Who Reads
- ☑ teacher
- ☐ students

Annotations (See page 58.)
- ☐ highlight main points
- ☐ circle key vocabulary
- ☐ underline key details
- ☐ arrows for connections
- ☐ write questions
- ☑ other: <u>box story elements (character, setting, problem, solution)</u>

Procedure

1. Tell students that they will listen to and read a story several times. Each time will be for a different purpose, to gain a better understanding of the story.

2. Display a copy of "Al's Choice" (page 152). Have students follow along as you read the passage aloud. Their goal is to get an overall idea of the story.

3. Ask students, "What is this passage about?"

4. After a brief discussion, ask students to follow along and try to understand more about the story as you read the text aloud.

5. **Partners**—After students have listened to you read the story, ask partners to briefly retell key details.

6. **Whole Class**—Regroup as a class, and display the text for all students. Ask students to share their responses to the initial question. Make annotations on your copy of the text.

7. If needed, ask additional layered/scaffolded questions, such as:
   - What name is in the title?
   - What is a choice?
   - Who has to make a choice?
   - How do the illustrations help you predict what choice Al will have to make?

8. Have students share any words that are challenging. Guide them to clarify the words throughout future readings.

Al's Choice *(cont.)*

Phase 2—Digging Deeper

Who Reads	Annotations (See page 58.)		
☑ teacher	☑ highlight main points	☑ underline key details	☐ write questions
☐ students	☐ circle key vocabulary	☐ arrows for connections	☑ other: <u>exclamation mark for solution</u>

Procedure

1. Use the annotated text from Phase 1 to review the two choices Al has to make in the story. Let the students identify that the choices are spending his money on a movie ticket and giving the ticket he finds back to the boy.

2. Ask students to give reasons *for* and *against* each choice.

3. Slowly read paragraphs 1–4 aloud, to allow students to listen for reasons for and against each choice. As they listen to the text, students will use annotations to identify key details that show the reasons for and the reasons against spending the money on a movie ticket.

4. If needed, ask additional layered/scaffolded questions, such as:
   · How does Al feel about seeing the movie? How do you know?
   · What did Al and his mom do to get the money for the movie tickets?
   · Why did Al help his neighbors?
   · What does "the right thing" mean?

5. **Partners**—After students have listened to and annotated the text, pairs can share their thinking as related to the reasons for and against Al spending his money on a movie ticket. Have partners list the reasons for and the reasons against Al spending his money on a movie ticket.

6. **Whole Class**—Regroup as a class, and display the text for all students. Ask students to share their responses to the question regarding Al's first problem. Have students support their responses with their annotations. If possible, record student annotations on a displayed copy of the text. You may also wish to create a two-columned anchor chart (similar to *What Should He Do?* on page 153) and label one column *for* and the other column *against*. List the reasons students provide in the appropriate column, and leave the chart on display for students to reference.

7. Provide time for students to return to the text and their own annotations and have them color code the details using two different colors, one designated as *for* and the other designated as *against*.

8. Have students return to the text one more time to identify how Al's problem is resolved. Read paragraph 5 aloud, and direct students to write an exclamation mark in the text where the problem is solved.

Phase 3—Going Even Deeper

Who Reads	Annotations (See page 58.)		
☐ teacher	☑ highlight main points	☐ underline key details	☐ write questions
☑ students	☐ circle key vocabulary	☐ arrows for connections	☐ other:_____

Procedure

1. Review the first choice Al makes. Then ask, "What is the next choice Al makes?"

2. Explain to students that they will listen to you read the last two paragraphs. Remind them of the text-dependent question *What are the reasons for and against Al's choices?* Have students use annotations to highlight the reasons *for* and *against* Al keeping the ticket. If desired, students can color code their annotations.

3. **Partners**—After students have read and annotated the text, pairs can share their annotations and thinking. Encourage students to discuss and provide text-based evidence for the following questions.

   - Why does Al think, *But maybe that boy wanted to see the movie as badly as I did. Maybe he had worked just has hard to earn the money?*
   - What do you learn about Al from this statement?

4. **Whole Class**—Regroup as a class, and display the text for all students. Ask students to share their responses to the questions. Have them support their responses with the annotations they have spoken, drawn, or dictated. If possible, record student annotations on a displayed copy of the text.

5. Provide students with the *What Should He Do?* activity (page 153). Direct students to review their annotations and sort the reasons for and against keeping the ticket Al found. Encourage students to work with partners as needed.

6. Pose the question *Why didn't the author tell what Al's choice was at the end of the story?* Explain that, in the performance assessment, students will use what they have learned about Al to predict what his choice will be.

Performance Assessment

1. Assign the performance task *What Will He Do?* (page 154).

2. Guide students to think about their work and complete the *What Will He Do? Reflection Page* (page 155).

Al's Choice

1   Al stopped in his tracks. The movie he wanted to see was finally out. And he even had money to buy a ticket. Well, the money was supposed to be for the baseball trip. That's where he was headed—to sign up for the trip. The money was right there in his pocket.

2   As soon as he heard about the trip, Al had begged to go. But his mom said they couldn't afford it. Al was so disappointed. He had spent the next couple of days sulking around the house.

3   "I see how unhappy you are," Al's mom had finally said. "Let's figure out a way to get the money." So his mom scrimped and saved for weeks, and to do his part, Al spent his spare time helping neighbors.

4   At the end of each week, Al and his mom counted the money until finally there was enough. Al was remembering all this as he stared at the movie theater. He couldn't spend the money on the movie. His mother trusted him to do the right thing.

5   Just then, a strong breeze blew, and a movie ticket landed right at his feet. Unbelievable! Al could see the movie *and* go on the trip. He scooped up the ticket and headed for the door. As he neared the theater, Al heard a boy frantically talking to the ticket taker. "But I bought a ticket! I just had it!" Al could tell the boy was holding back tears. Another gust of wind blew past the theater.

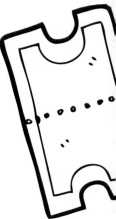

6   *Well, too bad for him*, Al thought. *He should have been more careful. But maybe he wants to see the movie as badly as I do. Maybe he had worked just as hard to earn the money.* Al made his choice. What would you do?

What Should He Do?

Directions: Al has a choice to make. Fill out the chart. List the reasons he should keep the ticket. List the reasons he should give it back.

For Keeping the Ticket

Against Keeping the Ticket (Giving It Back)

What Will He Do?

Directions: Do you think Al will give the movie ticket back? Do you think he will keep it? Fill Al's head with words from the story that help you decide. Complete the sentence below.

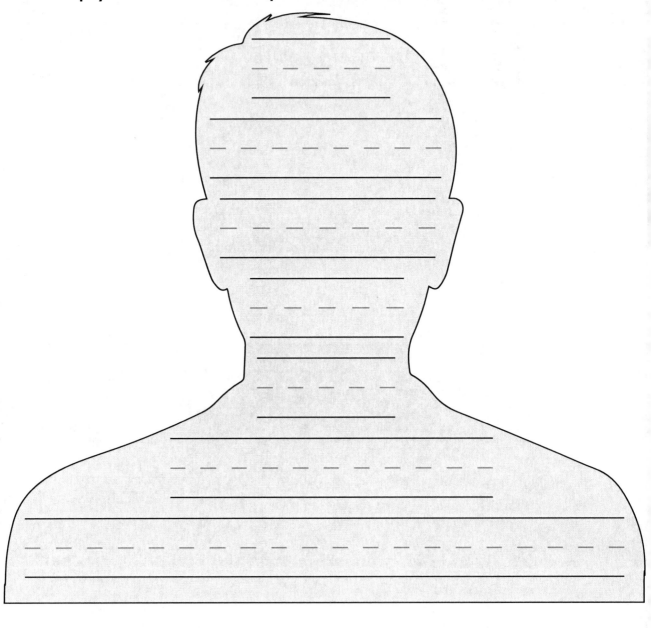

Al will _____ because _____ .

What Will He Do? Reflection Page

Directions: Think about your work. Did you follow directions? Circle the *thumbs up* or *thumbs down* picture for each part.

What I Think about My Work

	Yes	No
I chose words that show what choice Al will make.	👍	👎
My sentence has one clear reason.	👍	👎

Teacher comments: _____

_____

_____

_____

_____

Rubric based on work by Lapp, D., B. Moss, M. Grant, & K. Johnson (2015)

Alien in the Basement

Purpose

WHAT: Use illustrations to identify story elements.

HOW: Describe illustrations to retell a story.

I CAN: I can use illustrations to retell a story.

Standards

→ **Reading:** Use information from the illustrations and words to show comprehension of the text.

→ **Writing:** Write descriptions using key details.

→ **Language:** Use adjectives to add description.

Performance Assessment

→ Students will describe the illustrations that accompany the text to retell the story.

Text Selection

→ "Alien in the Basement"

→ The text is written in a graphic novel format.

Materials

→ *Alien in the Basement* passage, one copy per student (page 162; alienbasement.pdf)

→ *Just the Pictures* activity (page 163)

→ *Words and Pictures* activity (page 164)

→ *Words and Pictures Reflection Page* (page 165)

Text-Dependent Questions (See pages 46–48 for more information.)

→ What kind of text is this?

→ What is this text about?

→ What do the illustrations and text tell about the setting?

→ What do the illustrations and text tell about the characters?

→ What evidence is there that the alien is a person?

Alien in the Basement *(cont.)*

Areas of Complexity

	Measure	Explanation
Quantitative	Lexile Level	390L
Qualitative	Meaning or Purpose	This text is told in the format of a graphic novel and tells a story of one brother trying to trick another brother with no success. The dialog is purposefully deceitful with clues about what is actually happening.
	Structure	The text is written in panels with some dialog. A flashback is depicted in one panel.
	Language Features	Conventional and everyday language is used throughout.
Reader/ Task	Knowledge Demands	Some students may not be familiar with the setting of a basement. Students must identify details from the text and from the illustrations to complete the performance task.

Text Synopsis

Trevor hears a noise in the basement. As Trevor investigates further, an alien informs Trevor that he is hungry for a little brother or a brownie. Trevor remembers the brownies that were served for dessert and that his brother ate one, but Trevor has half of one saved. As Trevor turns on the lights, he sees someone running to hide. Not willing to give up his half brownie, Trevor tells the alien to get back in his spaceship.

Differentiation

Additional Support—Build background to support students' understanding of a basement. Pictures or other visual aids may be useful to help students understand this setting. Also, discussing each panel one at a time may help students better understand the plot.

Extension—Have students write what happens the next time Trevor's brother tries to trick him. Students can create their scenario in graphic novel format.

Phase 1—Hitting the Surface

Who Reads	Annotations (See page 59.)		
☑ teacher	☑ highlight main points	☐ underline key details	☐ write questions
☑ students	☐ circle key vocabulary	☐ arrows for connections	☐ other: _____

Procedure

1. Tell students that they will read a story several times. Each time will be for a different purpose, to gain a better understanding of the story.

2. Have students read and annotate the passage to get an overall idea of the story to answer the question *What is this story about?*

3. After students have read and annotated the text once, let them know you will read the text aloud. Have students follow along as you read the text, and have them mark the main idea and key details.

4. **Partners**—After students have listened to you read the story, ask partners to briefly retell the story.

5. If needed, ask additional layered/scaffolded questions, such as:
   - Who are the characters?
   - What is the setting?
   - What happens in the beginning, middle, and end?

6. **Whole Class**—Regroup as a class, and display "Alien in the Basement" (page 162) for all students. Ask students to share their responses to the question regarding what the story is about. Have them support their responses with their annotations. If possible, record student annotations on a displayed copy of the text.

7. Discuss the format of the text. Identify other kinds of texts that are written in this format, such as graphic novels, comic books, and comic strips. Discuss how students will read the text—each panel one at a time from left to right, or from top to bottom. If needed, ask additional layered/scaffolded questions, such as:
   - How are the illustrations laid out?
   - How is the text laid out?
   - What kind of text is this?

8. Students should also bring any challenging words to your attention. Guide students to use context clues to clarify key words throughout subsequent readings.

Alien in the Basement *(cont.)*

Phase 2—Digging Deeper

Who Reads	Annotations (See page 59.)		
❏ teacher	❏ highlight main points	☑ underline key details	❏ write questions
☑ students	❏ circle key vocabulary	❏ arrows for connections	❏ other:_____

Procedure

1. Review with students that they now have a general idea of the format of the text and what the text is about. In this phase of the lesson, they will reread to gain a better understanding of the text. Quickly review story elements found in most fiction texts: characters, setting, plot (sequence of events). Let students identify these. Tell students that they will reread the text to answer the question *What do the words and illustrations tell about the setting?*

2. **Partners**—Have partners work together to identify details in the words and illustrations that tell more about the setting. Encourage students to annotate the text by underlining key details and drawing arrows for making connections. If needed, ask additional layered/scaffolded questions, such as:
   - What name is used in the text?
   - Who is Trevor talking to in the text?
   - What characters are shown in the illustrations?
   - What details are included in the illustrations, but not in the words?

3. If needed, provide a model:
   - Say, "I see in the illustration that Trevor is at the top of the stairs. Behind him I can see the inside of his house. It looks like he is looking down into a basement. It is dark in the basement, so the lights probably aren't on." Circle the doorway that Trevor is standing in and the stairs in the illustration of the first panel.

4. **Whole Group**—Regroup as a class, and discuss students' findings about the setting. Create a two-columned chart with the name of each character listed at the top. List details that students share in the correct column to show details for each character. Write the letter *I* to the side of details found in the illustrations and *T* to the side of details found in the text.

Phase 3—Going Even Deeper

Who Reads

☐ teacher

☑ students

Annotations (See page 59.)

☐ highlight main points ☑ underline key details ☐ write questions

☐ circle key vocabulary ☑ arrows for connections ☐ other:_____

Procedure

1. Tell students they will dig deeper into "Alien in the Basement" by looking closely at the illustrations and the text together to answer questions about the story.

2. Have students reread the text to answer the question *What evidence is there that the alien is a person?* Encourage students to annotate the text by underlining key details and drawing arrows to make connections. Remind students to use both the text and illustrations for clues to help them answer the question.

3. **Partners**—After students have read and annotated the text once, pairs can share their thinking as related to the initial question. Ask layered/scaffolded questions, such as:
   - What is the alien hungry for in panel 2?
   - Who ate brownies together in panel 3?
   - What part of the alien can be seen in the illustration of panel 5?

4. **Whole Class**—Regroup as a class, and display the text for all students. Ask students to share their responses to the question regarding who the alien is. Have them support their responses with their annotations. If possible, record student annotations on a displayed copy of the text. Reinforce the evidence in the text and illustrations to show the answer to the question.

5. Provide students with copies of the *Just the Pictures* activity (page 163). Explain that good readers use the illustrations to help them make sense of the story. In this practice page, they will describe what they see in the illustrations of this story. Allow students to work individually or with partners to complete the activity.

6. **Whole Class**—Gather back together to discuss students' responses to *Just the Pictures*. Provide a sticky note to each student. Have them cover the text of each panel as one student reads his/her findings. Ask the other students if they can find evidence of the details in only the pictures. Allow students to revise their ideas as needed.

Performance Assessment

1. Assign the performance task *Words and Pictures* (page 164).

2. Guide students to think about their work and complete the *Words and Pictures Reflection Page* (page 165).

Alien in the Basement

1 Trevor heard a noise. It was coming from the basement.

"Stop or I will eat you!" a voice hissed from below.

2 Trevor bravely moved down the stairs. "Who are you?" he asked.

"I am an alien!" the voice replied, "And I am hungry for a little brother...or an Earth brownie.

3 Trevor stopped. Brownie? He thought back to dessert. His brother ate a brownie. Trevor had saved half of his brownie in the fridge.

4 Trevor walked slowly up the stairs.

"This is your last chance," said the voice. "Bring me an Earth brownie or I will eat-"

5 Trevor flipped the light switch and the basement become bright.

CLICK

"Nooooo! I'm allergic to Earth light," said the voice.

6 "Time to get back in your spaceship, alien," Trevor said. "I'm keeping my brownie."

Trevor saw a blur of something running to hide behind the laundry basket.

Just the Pictures

Directions: Retell the story. Write a sentence to describe each panel. The first panel has been done for you.

Panel 1
A boy is a standing at the top of the stairs. The stairs go down to a dark basement.
Panel 2
_____ _____
Panel 3
_____ _____
Panel 4
_____ _____
Panel 5
_____ _____
Panel 6
_____ _____

Words and Pictures

Directions: Choose a panel. In the first row, write a detail that is only in the text. In the second row, write a detail that is only in the pictures. In the last row, write a detail you can find in both the text and pictures.

	Panel # _____
Text	
Illustrations	
Both	

Words and Pictures Reflection Page

Directions: Think about your work. Write a check mark in the *Yes* or *No* column to show if you did all of the parts of the project.

What I Think about My Work

	Yes	No
I described a detail I found only in the text.		
I described a detail I found only in the pictures.		
I described a detail I found in both the text and pictures.		

Teacher comments: _____

_____

_____

_____

_____

Rubric based on work by Lapp, D., B. Moss, M. Grant, & K. Johnson (2015)

Try It!

Use the passage below and the planning forms that follow to plan a close reading lesson.

The Mighty Tree and the Little Plant (510L)

At the forest's edge stood a huge tree. Its branches were spread wide. Its roots were deep. A little plant grew at the foot of the tree. A little breeze caused it to bend.

The big tree and the little plant spoke. Each was worried about how they would survive the winter.

"Why can't your roots grow deeper into the ground like mine?" asked the tree. "Why can't you raise your head into the air like me?"

The plant looked at the tree's branches and said, "I feel safer down here."

The tree's laughter shook the ground, "You can't be safer than me! My trunk is thick and strong!"

That night, a terrible storm came. The little plant was blown this way and that. "I won't survive!" he cried.

But when morning came, the little plant found he had survived. He straightened his leaves and looked to see the tree, only to find the tree had fallen!

Try It! *(cont.)*

Planning Chart for Close Reading

Planning

Date: _____ Grade: _____ Discipline: _____

Purpose(s): _____

Standard(s): _____

Text Selection (literary or informational): _____

Performance Assessment: _____

Materials: _____

Text Selection

Title: _____

Author: _____

Page(s) or Section(s): _____

How should this text be chunked? _____

_____

Areas of Complexity

Lexile Level: _____

Meaning or Purpose: _____

Structure: _____

Language Features: _____

Knowledge Demands: _____

Text-Dependent Questions

1. _____

2. _____

3. _____

4. _____

5. _____

Performance Task

_____

_____

_____

_____

Differentiation

Additional Support: _____

_____

Extension: _____

Try It! *(cont.)*

Teaching Close Reading

Teaching

Limited Frontloading ❏ yes ❏ no

Describe:

First Read

Who Reads? ❏ teacher ❏ student

Student Materials

❏ graphic organizer

❏ note taking guide

❏ group consensus form

❏ summary form

Second Read

Who Reads? ❏ teacher ❏ student

Student Resources

❏ graphic organizer

❏ note taking guide

❏ group consensus form

❏ summary form

Additional Reads

Who Reads? ❏ teacher ❏ student

Student Resources

❏ graphic organizer

❏ note taking guide

❏ group consensus form

❏ summary form

Extension

Reteaching

Section 6:
Informational Text Close Reading Lessons

In the following pages, you will find nine close reading lessons built around informational texts. A tenth text is provided along with planning resources to allow you to plan an additional close reading lesson.

Key Ideas and Details Kindergarten Lesson 171

Key Ideas and Details Grade 1 Lesson 181

Key Ideas and Details Grade 2 Lesson 191

Craft and Structure Kindergarten Lesson 201

Craft and Structure Grade 1 Lesson. 211

Craft and Structure Grade 2 Lesson. 221

Integration of Knowledge and Ideas Kindergarten Lesson 231

Integration of Knowledge and Ideas Grade 1 Lesson 241

Integration of Knowledge and Ideas Grade 2 Lesson. 251

Try It! 260

Playing It Safe

Purpose

WHAT: Describe the main idea in a text.

HOW: Connect the main idea to real-life examples.

I CAN: I can use the main idea of a text in my real life.

Standards

→ **Reading:** With guidance and support, use the structure of the text to identify main idea and details.

→ **Writing:** With guidance and support, draw, write, or dictate using information from a text.

→ **Language:** Use academic words and phrases acquired through conversations, reading, and being read to when responding to texts.

Performance Assessment

→ Students will dictate and present statements about how they will stay safe at school.

Text Selection

→ "Playing It Safe"

→ Text is written in two paragraphs.

Materials

→ *Playing It Safe* passage, one copy per student (page 176; playingitsafe.pdf)

→ *Wear Your Gear* activity (page 177)

→ *Safety Promise* activity (page 178)

→ *Safety Promise Reflection Page* (page 179)

Text-Dependent Questions (See pages 40–42 for more information.)

→ What is the text about?

→ What is the main idea?

→ What details tell more about the main idea?

→ What examples tell more about the main idea?

Playing It Safe *(cont.)*

Areas of Complexity

	Measure	Explanation
Quantitative	Lexile Level	380L
Qualitative	Meaning or Purpose	This informational text tells about ways to stay safe while playing sports.
	Structure	The passage follows a main idea, supporting detail, and example structure that is standard for beginning readers.
	Language Features	Vocabulary that is specific to the topic of sports is used in the text.
Reader/ Task	Knowledge Demands	Students must differentiate between main idea, details, and examples that are all provided within the passage. Students must use examples from the text to complete the performance task.

Text Synopsis

Playing sports is fun, but getting hurt isn't! This informational text explains ways to stay safe by using protective gear and warming up. Examples of each are provided.

Differentiation

Additional Support—Create an anchor chart to display in the classroom of equipment that can be used to help stay safe while playing sports. Encourage students who participate in sports to share about what equipment they use. Add their ideas to the chart.

Extension—Have students identify other ways to stay safe while playing specific sports. For example, if students choose the sport of soccer, they can describe specialized equipment needed to play soccer safely.

Playing It Safe *(cont.)*

Phase 1—Hitting the Surface

Who Reads

☑ teacher

☐ students

Annotations (See page 58.)

☑ highlight main points   ☑ underline key details   ☐ write questions

☑ circle key vocabulary   ☐ arrows for connections   ☐ other: _____

Procedure

1. Tell students that they will listen to a text several times. Each time will be for a different purpose, to gain a better understanding of the text.

2. Display a copy of "Playing It Safe" (page 176). Have students listen as you read the passage to get an overall idea of the story.

3. Ask students to think about this question as you read: *What is this passage about?*

4. **Partners**—After students have listened to you read the text once, ask partners to share what they think the text is about.

5. **Whole Class**—Regroup as a class, and display the text for all students. Ask students to share their responses to the initial question. Make annotations on your copy of the text.

Phase 2—Digging Deeper

Who Reads

☑ teacher

☐ students

Annotations (See page 58.)

☑ highlight main points   ☐ underline key details   ☐ write questions

☑ circle key vocabulary   ☐ arrows for connections   ☐ other: _____

Procedure

1. Tell students that they will listen to the text again to understand more about the main idea.

2. Review that the main idea is what the text is mostly about. Read aloud the entire text to students again. As you read, students should listen for the answer to the question *What is the main idea of the text?*

Playing It Safe (cont.)

Phase 2—Digging Deeper (cont.)

Procedure (cont.)

3. Tell students that sometimes there may be words in texts that they know only a little or don't understand at all. Slowly reread the text aloud to students. Have students raise their hands when you come to words they do not know. Have individual students circle those unfamiliar words on the displayed text. Guide students to use strategies for determining the meanings of the unknown words. For example, students may hear the word *protect* in the word *protective*.

4. Support students in finding the main idea by asking additional layered/scaffolded questions about the text, such as:
   - What is the title?
   - What is the first sentence about?
   - What is this passage mostly about?
   - Does the rest of the passage tell more about the main idea?

5. **Partners**—Ask partners to share their thinking answers about the text-dependent questions in steps 3 and 4.

6. **Whole Class**—Regroup as a class, and display the text for all students. Ask students to share the main idea they identified. Once again, have students annotate the displayed copy of the text.

Phase 3—Going Even Deeper

Who Reads	Annotations (See page 58.)		
☑ teacher	☐ highlight main points	☐ underline key details	☐ write questions
☐ students	☑ circle key vocabulary	☐ arrows for connections	☑ other: <u>color-code main idea, details, and examples</u>

Procedure

1. Remind students of the main idea they identified. Explain that the ideas that follow in the passage are called *details* and tell more about the main idea. Tell students that this time, as they listen to the text, they should listen for details that tell more about the main idea.

2. Reread the text, and have students listen for the answer to the question *What details tell more about the main idea?*

Phase 3—Going Even Deeper *(cont.)*

Procedure *(cont.)*

3. If needed, ask additional layered/scaffolded questions, such as:
   - What tells more about staying safe while playing sports?
   - How does the helmet detail tell more about staying safe?
   - How does the stretching detail tell more about staying safe?

4. **Partners**—Ask partners to share their thinking about the details of the text. Have students identify how the details tell more about the main idea by asking *How does this tell more about staying safe while playing sports?*

5. **Whole Class**—Regroup as a class, and display the text for all students. Ask students to share the details they identified. Once again, have students make annotations on the displayed copy of the text.

6. Explain that the text provides specific examples that support the key details in the text. Have students complete the *Wear Your Gear* activity (page 177) individually or with partners to identify specific examples listed in the text.

7. Display a clean copy of the text for all students to see. Read the first paragraph again to students. Underline the main idea of the text using a green marker. Underline the supporting details of the text using a yellow marker. Underline the examples for each supporting detail in red.

8. Ask students to listen to the second paragraph for a similar pattern. Read the second paragraph aloud. Allow students to highlight the main idea, details, and examples in green, yellow, and red, respectively. Tell students that this is a structure that many informational texts follow.

Performance Assessment

1. Assign the performance task *Safety Promise* (page 178). Have students state their safety promise sentences to the class.

2. Guide students to think about their work and complete the *Safety Promise Reflection Page* (page 179).

Playing It Safe

1   It's good to play sports, but it's not good to get hurt. To stay safe, remember to wear protective gear. Helmets are a good idea. Elbow pads and kneepads also help. Make sure you use the right kind of gear for your sport.

2   Remember to warm up. Jog a little bit, and then do some stretching. Warm muscles won't get hurt as easily. If you get injured, stop and rest. You may need to see a doctor.

Wear Your Gear

Directions: Color the things that keep the skaters safe.

Protective Gear

Safety Promise

Directions: Make a promise to be safe at recess. Use words and ideas from the text. An adult will help you draw and write your promise.

I will stay ᔕᗩᖴᗴ by _____

_____

_____

_____ .

Safety Promise Reflection Page

Directions: Think about your work. Did you follow directions? Circle the *thumbs up* or *thumbs down* picture for each part.

What I Think about My Work

	Yes	No
I used a word from the text.	👍	👎
I used a safety idea from the text.	👍	👎
My promise is something that will keep me safe.	👍	👎

Teacher comments: _____

_____

_____

_____

_____

_____

Rubric based on work by Lapp, D., B. Moss, M. Grant, & K. Johnson (2015)

On the Wire

Purpose

WHAT: Identify the key details of an informational text.

HOW: Create an ad that describes the main event of a story.

I CAN: I can summarize key details of an informational text.

Standards

→ **Reading:** Identify key details in a text.

→ **Writing:** Write an opinion including some details to support the opinion.

→ **Language:** Understand the use of proper nouns.

Performance Assessment

→ Students will create an advertisement to encourage coming to see the show Philippe Petit will put on.

Text Selection

→ "On the Wire"

→ Text is organized into five paragraphs describing an event.

Materials

→ *On the Wire* passage, one copy per student (page 186; onthewire.pdf)

→ *What a Show!* activity (page 187)

→ *Come One, Come All!* activity (page 188)

→ *Come One, Come All! Reflection Page* (page 189)

Text-Dependent Questions (See pages 43–45 for more information.)

→ What is the text about?

→ Why is the setting important to this text?

→ What details tell how the viewers reacted?

→ Why did the author write this text?

On the Wire (cont.)

Areas of Complexity

	Measure	Explanation
Quantitative	Lexile Level	530L
Qualitative	Meaning or Purpose	This informational text tells about a wirewalker who illegally walked between the Twin Towers in New York.
	Structure	The passage follows the sequence of what happened, with each paragraph describing an aspect of the event supported by key details. Elements of drama interrupt the typical sequence of narrative nonfiction.
	Language Features	Specific names of places students may not be familiar with are mentioned in this text. Additionally, precise vocabulary is used throughout.
Reader/Task	Knowledge Demands	Students must have background knowledge of how high a skyscraper is or will have to use details to understand where the setting is in order to understand Petit's courage/foolishness. Students must comprehend key details to complete the performance task.

Text Synopsis

On August 7, 1974, Philippe Petit walked on a cable 1,368 feet off the ground between the two buildings of the Twin Towers of New York. This passage describes his actions, the crowd's reactions, and ultimately the police reaction to his stunt. The reader is left to ponder if it was an act of courage or foolishness.

Differentiation

Additional Support—Help students who are struggling to understand the setting through a guided drawing of the Twin Towers and where the cable was located as you reread the first paragraph with them. Additional support can be to lay a piece of string/yarn down on the ground and reread the third paragraph as students act out what is being described. Ask students to imagine doing those actions 1,368 feet off the ground!

Extension—Have students write their opinions about whether Philippe Petit was courageous or foolish in paragraph form to respond to the last paragraph of the text.

On the Wire (cont.)

Phase 1—Hitting the Surface

Who Reads	Annotations (See page 58.)		
☑ teacher	☐ highlight main points	☐ underline key details	☐ write questions
☑ students	☐ circle key vocabulary	☐ arrows for connections	☐ other: _____

Procedure

1. Tell students that they will listen to and read a passage several times. Each time will be for a different purpose, to gain a better understanding of the text.

2. Display a copy of "On the Wire" (page 186) Have students follow along as you read the passage aloud. Their goal is to get an overall idea of the text.

3. Ask students, "What is this text about?"

4. After a brief discussion, ask students to follow along and try to understand more about the story as you read the text aloud again.

5. **Partners**—After students have listened to you read the passage, ask partners to briefly retell key details and circle any unfamiliar words they would like to understand better.

6. **Whole Class**—Regroup as a class, and display the text for all students. Ask students to share their responses to the initial question. Make annotations on your copy of the text.

7. If needed, ask additional layered/scaffolded questions, such as:
   - Does the text tell a story or provide information?
   - How is the text organized?
   - Who is the text about?
   - What is the setting?

8. Have students share any words that are challenging. Guide them to clarify the words throughout future readings.

Phase 2—Digging Deeper

Who Reads	Annotations (See page 58.)		
☐ teacher	☐ highlight main points	☑ underline key details	☐ write questions
☑ students	☐ circle key vocabulary	☐ arrows for connections	☐ other: _____

On the Wire *(cont.)*

Phase 2—Digging Deeper *(cont.)*

Procedure

1. Explain that you will read the text again so that students can understand the details in more depth.

2. Review with students that a setting is where and when an event happens. Sometimes there is one setting, sometimes multiple settings, and sometimes the setting changes. Tell students they will reread the first paragraph to find out more about the setting to answer the question *Why is the setting important to this text?*

3. Display the passage for students to see. Reread the first sentence aloud. Have students think about how the sentence can answer the question. For example, say, "I see the first sentence tells that the setting is the Twin Towers of the World Trade Center in New York. I notice that these all have capital letters, so they must be the names of places. This tells me about part of the setting. I don't really know what the Twin Towers are, but I can look for more details in the paragraph to help me understand."

4. Have students reread the rest of the first paragraph. They will then guide you to annotate the details that tell more about what the setting is and why they are important to the text.

5. **Partners**—After students have listened to and helped annotate the displayed text, pairs can share their thinking related to the question about the setting. If needed, ask additional layered/scaffolded questions, such as:
   - What does the word *twin* mean?
   - What words describe the Twin Towers?
   - How high up is the cable?

6. **Whole Class**—Regroup as a class, and display the text for all students. Ask students to share their responses to the question regarding the setting. Have them support their responses with their annotations. If possible, record student annotations on a displayed copy of the text. As a class, discuss why the setting is so important to this text. Could this have taken place anywhere else, for example on the ground?

7. Reread the final paragraph aloud. Discuss with students their opinions about whether Philippe Petit's wirewalk was an act of courage or silly danger. Have students defend their arguments with evidence from the text, in particular the setting.

Phase 3—Going Even Deeper

Who Reads	Annotations (See page 58.)		
☑ teacher	☑ highlight main points	☑ underline key details	☐ write questions
☑ students	☐ circle key vocabulary	☑ arrows for connections	☐ other:_____

Procedure

1. Tell students that they will reread the text to discover more about how it is organized.

2. Display a copy of the text for students to see. Point to and count the paragraphs in the text. Explain that authors usually group information together into paragraphs. Tell them that they will reread a paragraph to see how the information is grouped in this text.

3. Read aloud the second paragraph. Tell students that you notice that all the information in this paragraph describes what the people watching were doing. Ask students to listen to the second paragraph to answer the question *What details tell how the viewers reacted?* Have students annotate the displayed text by drawing arrows to show connections between the people watching and the words that describe their reactions.

4. **Partners**—Student pairs can share their thinking as related to the question about what the people who were watching were doing. If needed, ask additional layered/scaffolded questions, such as:
   - What other words are used for the people who were watching?
   - What sounds did they make?
   - How did they react with their bodies?

5. **Whole Class**—Regroup as a class, and display the text for all students. Ask students to share their responses.

6. Read aloud the fourth paragraph. Tell students that you notice all the information in this paragraph is about how unusual Philippe's act was.

7. On chart paper, recreate the *What a Show!* activity on page 187. Model the *What a Show!* activity on the chart paper as students complete the activity on their own copies of the activity.

Performance Assessment

1. Assign the performance task *Come One, Come All!* (page 188).

2. Guide students to think about their work and complete the *Come One, Come All! Reflection Page* (page 189).

On the Wire

1 The Twin Towers of the World Trade Center watched over New York City for 35 years. They stood like two giant guards, strong and quiet. But on August 7, 1974, people noticed something strange. There was a cable stretched between the buildings. Standing in the middle of the cable was a man. Philippe Petit was a master of the wirewalk. And he was walking on a cable between the two buildings! There was nothing between Petit and the ground except a fall of 1,368 feet.

2 As people held their breath, Petit placed one foot in front of the other. Viewers gasped. They cheered. They covered their eyes and peeked between their fingers.

3 Step by step, Petit did it. He reached the other side. And he reached it again. And again. Petit crossed eight times. He also lay down on the cable, danced, and leaped with both feet in the air!

4 Of course, the police were waiting for him. It wasn't legal to walk a tight wire between the towers. But Petit had done something almost no person on the planet could do. Most people would not even dream of doing it!

5 Amazing? Yes, it was. But was it an amazing act of courage or of silly danger? That is for you to decide.

What a Show!

Directions: Reread paragraph four. Use words from the text to describe what Philippe Petit did.

What Philippe Did

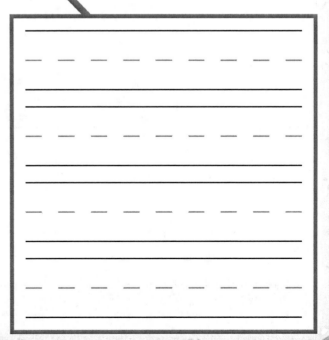

Come One, Come All!

Directions: Draw a poster to invite people to come see Philippe Petit's show. Tell when and where the show will be happen. Tell what they will see.

_____

- -

_____

- -

_____

Name:_____ Date: _____

Come One, Come All! Reflection Page

Directions: Think about your work. Did you follow directions?
Circle the *thumbs up* or *thumbs down* picture for each part.

What I Think about My Work

	Yes	No
My poster includes words to tell **when** the show will happen.	👍	👎
My poster includes words to tell **where** the show will happen.	👍	👎
My poster includes words to tell **what** will be seen.	👍	👎

Teacher comments: _____

_____

_____

_____

_____

_____

_____

_____

Rubric based on work by Lapp, D., B. Moss, M. Grant, & K. Johnson (2015)

Flying into Adventure

Purpose

WHAT: Summarize the main idea of the text.

HOW: Create a poster using information from the text.

I CAN: I can summarize the main idea of the text.

Standards

→ **Reading:** Identify the main idea and focus of each paragraph.

→ **Writing:** Write based on information gathered from a provided source.

→ **Language:** Determine the meaning of words with prefixes.

Performance Assessment

→ Students will create a "missing" poster using information from the text.

Text Selection

→ "Flying into Adventure"

→ Text is organized into paragraphs. It includes a photograph and time line that support the text.

Materials

→ *Flying into Adventure* passage, one copy per student (page 196; adventure.pdf)

→ *Find the Focus* activity (page 197)

→ *Missing* activity (page 198)

→ *Missing Reflection Page* (page 199)

Text-Dependent Questions (See pages 46–48 for more information.)

→ What is the text about?

→ What kind of text is this?

→ How do the prefixes in the text help you figure out unknown words?

→ What is the focus of each paragraph?

→ What is the main idea?

Flying into Adventure *(cont.)*

Areas of Complexity

	Measure	Explanation
Quantitative	Lexile Level	580L
Qualitative	Meaning or Purpose	This text is a short biography of Amelia Earhart. Earhart's accomplishments are chronicled sequentially with additional details about the era.
	Structure	The text is organized into paragraphs and follows the sequence of Amelia Earhart's life. A photograph and time line are provided as supporting features.
	Language Features	The language is conventional. Some precise words are used throughout but should not interfere with overall understanding. Several words have prefixes.
Reader/ Task	Knowledge Demands	The text requires that students have a basic understanding that a biography tells the story of a real person's life. Students must select key details from the text to complete the performance task.

Text Synopsis

Amelia Earhart was a woman who did what she loved—flying. From the first time she saw an airplane, she was hooked. She was the first woman to fly across the Atlantic Ocean, first woman to fly solo across the Atlantic Ocean, and attempted to be the first woman to fly around the world. Her plane never made it, and she was never found. Even so, she is still admired today for her bravery.

Differentiation

Additional Support—Ask additional scaffolded questions to guide students to understand the text. Scaffolded questions can include the *W* questions, such as:

- When did Amelia learn to fly?
- What was she the first woman to do?
- Where was she when she disappeared?
- Why do people think she is brave?

If needed, direct students to specific paragraphs to answer each question.

Extension—Have students think or write about whether or not they would be brave enough to do the things Amelia Earhart did. Discuss how difficult it is to be the first one to do something and to be determined when people are saying something cannot be done.

Flying into Adventure (cont.)

Phase 1—Hitting the Surface

Who Reads

☑ teacher
☑ students

Annotations (See page 59.)

☑ highlight main points ☑ underline key details ☑ write questions
☑ circle key vocabulary ☑ arrows for connections ☐ other: _____

Procedure

1. Tell students that they will read a text several times. Each time will be for a different purpose, to gain a better understanding of the information.

2. Have students read and annotate "Flying into Adventure" (page 196) to get an overall idea of the text to answer the question *What is this text about?*

3. After students have read and annotated the text once, let them know you will read the text aloud. Have students follow along and mark the main idea and key details as you read.

4. **Partners**—After students have listened to you read the story, ask partners to briefly retell the main idea and key details.
   · Who is this text about?
   · Does this text tell a story or provide information?
   · What is Amelia Earhart known for?
   · How do the photograph and time line relate to the text?

5. **Whole Class**—Regroup as a class, and display the text for all students. Ask students to share their responses to the question regarding what the text is about. Have them support their responses with their annotations. If possible, record student annotations on a displayed copy of the text.

6. Ask students to skim the text again to find the years that are listed on the time line. Have them annotate the text by putting a box around the years and drawing arrows to the time line to show the connection of the time line to each paragraph.

7. Students should also bring any challenging words to your attention. Guide students to use context clues to clarify key words throughout subsequent readings.

Phase 2—Digging Deeper

Who Reads

☐ teacher
☑ students

Annotations (See page 59.)

☐ highlight main points ☐ underline key details ☐ write questions
☑ circle key vocabulary ☐ arrows for connections ☐ other: _____

Flying into Adventure *(cont.)*

Phase 2—Digging Deeper *(cont.)*

Procedure

1. Explain to students that they will dig deeper into the text during this phase of the lesson to understand some of the words that help explain the details in the text.

2. Display the text, and reread the first paragraph. Model using prefixes to clarify words as you read:

   - Say, "I will circle the word *unable* in the first paragraph because I am not sure what it means. I see the word *able* in the word and know that the prefix *un-* means 'not' or 'opposite,' so *unable* must mean 'not able.'"
   - Reread the sentence, substituting *not able* for *unable* to show students that it makes sense in context.
   - Make a list of any other prefixes students are familiar with and their meanings. Ensure *un-* and *re-* are on the list.

3. Have students reread the text to answer the question *How do the prefixes in the text help you figure out unknown words?* Ask students to annotate the text by circling any words with prefixes.

4. **Partners**—After students have read and annotated the text, pairs can share the words they located and what they determined the words mean.

5. **Whole Class**—Regroup as a class, and display the text for all students. Ask students to share the vocabulary words they found. Create a chart with columns labeled *Word*, *Prefix*, *Root Word*, and *Meaning*. Add words and information to the chart as students share their responses.

6. Now that students are more familiar with the meanings of the words from the word study above, have students reread the text independently.

Phase 3—Going Even Deeper

Who Reads	Annotations (See page 59.)		
☐ teacher	☐ highlight main points	☐ underline key details	☐ write questions
☑ students	☐ circle key vocabulary	☑ arrows for connections	☐ other: _____

Procedure

1. Return to the text, and remind students that each time they read a text for a different purpose, they gain a better understanding of the text. This time, they will read to find out more about how the text is organized.

Phase 3—Going Even Deeper *(cont.)*

Procedure *(cont.)*

2. Display a copy of the text for students. Say, "Authors usually group similar information together. Sometimes, authors even describe the focus of the paragraph in the first sentence of the paragraph." Use the following think-aloud to model annotating the first paragraph. Say, "I see that the text says she was a brave woman in the first sentence. Then, in the second sentence, it says she loved flying. You have to be brave in order to fly, so I am going to draw an arrow from the word *flying* back to the word *brave*. I also read that Amelia did not care what other people thought. You have to be brave to do that, too. I'm going to draw an arrow from the phrase *did not care what they thought* back to the word *brave* in the first sentence."

3. After annotating the first paragraph, identify the focus as *bravery*. Write the word *bravery* in the margin of the text.

4. Provide students with *Find the Focus* activity (page 197). Have students answer the question *What is the focus of each paragraph?* Have them annotate each paragraph by drawing arrows for connections they make within each paragraph. After they are done with each paragraph, have students identify a focus for the paragraph with a word or a short phrase. Have them write in the empty box at the top of each paragraph.

5. **Partners**—After students have completed their reads and annotated the text once, have pairs share their thinking related to the question *What is the focus of each paragraph?*

6. **Whole Class**—Regroup as a class, and display the text for all students. Ask students to share their responses to the question regarding what the text is about. Have them support their responses with their annotations. If possible, record student annotations on a displayed copy of the text.

7. Have students look at the focus of all of the paragraphs. Explain that the main idea is a thought that has to do with all the paragraphs of a text. Have students look at the focuses they wrote for each paragraph to answer the question *What idea do all the paragraphs support?* Have students look for a unifying idea among all the paragraphs.

8. Tell students that the title often, but not always, tells about the main idea. Read the title aloud. Discuss with students whether it is the main idea and if it is a good title. Have pairs work together to write another title that tells the main idea. If desired, write each idea on a sheet of chart paper, including the actual title of the text, and have students vote on the title they think most accurately describes the main idea of the text.

Performance Assessment

1. Assign the performance task *Missing* (page 198).

2. Guide students to think about their work and complete the *Missing Reflection Page* (page 199).

Flying into Adventure

1 Amelia Earhart was a brave woman. She loved flying. Many people in her time thought women were unable to fly. Amelia did not care what they thought. She did what she loved.

2 Amelia was born in Kansas in 1897. One day, she went to an air show. She saw an airplane zoom near her. She was thrilled by the sight. Soon, she learned to fly.

3 One day, a man asked if she wanted to be the first woman to fly across the Atlantic Ocean. Of course she did! In 1928, she became the first woman to make the trip as a passenger.

4 Then, Amelia planned a solo trip across the ocean. Many people said a woman could not do it. But Amelia made up her mind. She made her solo flight in 1932. Harsh weather made it hard to fly. But she crossed the Atlantic Ocean alone!

5 Amelia wanted to be the first woman to fly around the world. In 1937, she and a friend began the trip. They made it almost all the way. They landed to refuel the airplane. Then, they headed to a tiny island called Howland Island. Unfortunately, the airplane never made it. People searched for Amelia for years. It is uncertain what happened to her and the plane. Everyone hoped she would reappear someday.

6 Amelia believed in herself. She knew she was strong, smart, and brave. She did not listen when people said she could not do something. She proved that women could do the same things men could do. That is why people admire her today.

7 1897: Born in Kansas

8 1928: First flight across the Atlantic Ocean as a passenger

9 1932: First solo flight across the Atlantic Ocean

10 1937: Crash location

Find the Focus

Directions: What is each paragraph mostly about? Write a short note in each box to tell the focus.

Flying into Adventure

```
┌──────────────────────────────────────────────────────┐
│                                                      │
│                                                      │
└──────────────────────────────────────────────────────┘
```

Amelia Earhart was a brave woman. She loved flying. Many people in her time thought women were unable to fly. Amelia did not care what they thought. She did what she loved.

```
┌──────────────────────────────────────────────────────┐
│                                                      │
│                                                      │
└──────────────────────────────────────────────────────┘
```

Amelia was born in Kansas in 1897. One day, she went to an air show. She saw an airplane zoom near her. She was thrilled by the sight. Soon, she learned to fly.

```
┌──────────────────────────────────────────────────────┐
│                                                      │
│                                                      │
└──────────────────────────────────────────────────────┘
```

One day, a man asked if she wanted to be the first woman to fly across the Atlantic Ocean. Of course she did! In 1928, she became the first woman to make the trip as a passenger.

Missing

Directions: Create a "missing" poster for Amelia Earhart. Use information you learned from the text. Tell about Amelia's life. Tell about her disappearance.

MISSING

Missing Reflection Page

Directions: Think about your work. Write a check mark in the *Yes* or *No* column to show if you did all parts of the project.

What I Think about My Work

	Yes	No
My poster has information about Amelia Earhart's life.		
My poster has information about Amelia Earhart's disappearance.		
The information is from "Flying into Adventure."		
My poster is neat and shows creativity.		

Teacher comments: _____

_____

_____

_____

Rubric based on work by Lapp, D., B. Moss, M. Grant, & K. Johnson (2015)

Drip, Drop, Down

Purpose

WHAT: Describe the sequence of events presented in informational text.

HOW: Draw or write about the events of the water cycle.

I CAN: I can describe events in order.

Standards

→ **Reading:** With guidance and support, determine the meaning of unknown words in a text.

→ **Writing:** With guidance and support, draw, write, or talk about the water cycle.

→ **Language:** Use words acquired through reading when responding to texts.

→ **Science:** Describe the pattern of the water cycle.

Performance Assessment

→ Students will draw and write about what happens in the air and in the ground with the water cycle.

Text Selection

→ "Drip, Drop, Down"

→ Text is divided into paragraphs. It is sequenced to show the water cycle.

Materials

→ *Drip, Drop, Down* passage, one copy per student (page 206; dripdropdown.pdf)

→ *Water Cycle Word Sort* activity (page 207)

→ *Look Up and Down* activity (page 208)

→ *Look Up and Down Reflection Page* (page 209)

Text-Dependent Questions (See pages 40–42 for more information.)

→ What is this text about?

→ What kind of text is this?

→ How does the title relate to the text?

→ How does the author use science words to help us understand the water cycle?

→ How does the author explain the sequence of the water cycle?

Drip, Drop, Down (cont.)

Areas of Complexity

	Measure	Explanation
Quantitative	Lexile Level	310L
Qualitative	Meaning or Purpose	This informative text tells the sequence of the water cycle.
Qualitative	Structure	The passage follows the sequential text structure from one step to the next.
Qualitative	Language Features	The text contains challenging and specialized scientific vocabulary.
Reader/ Task	Knowledge Demands	Students must have some knowledge about the states of matter and that water can exist as more than just liquid. Students must group and sort details to complete the performance task.

Text Synopsis

We have the same water on Earth that we always have had. This text explains the process of how that water makes a cycle. The text describes the changes as water evaporates, forms clouds, rains or snows, and forms lakes and rivers. And then the process begins all over again.

Differentiation

Additional Support—Create a water cycle demonstration in the classroom. Fill a zipper-topped baggie with water and tape it in a window. Have students observe over time how the water evaporates and collects (condenses) at the top of the baggie and then drips back down toward the bottom of the baggie. This visual provides a concrete model for students to observe.

Extension—Have students draw pictures of the entire water cycle. Encourage them to use all the scientific words used in the passage as they label their pictures.

Drip, Drop, Down *(cont.)*

Phase 1—Hitting the Surface

Who Reads | Annotations (See page 58.)

☑ teacher ☐ highlight main points ☑ underline key details ☐ write questions

☐ students ☐ circle key vocabulary ☐ arrows for connections ☐ other: _____

Procedure

1. Tell students that they will listen to a text several times. Each time will be for a different purpose, to gain a better understanding of the text.

2. Display a copy of the text. Have students listen to you read the passage to get an overall idea of the story.

3. Ask students, "What is this text about?"

4. **Partners**—After students have listened to you read the text once, have partners share what they think the text is about.

5. **Whole Class**—Regroup as a class, and display the text for all students. Have students share their responses to the initial question. Make annotations on your copy of the text.

Drip, Drop, Down *(cont.)*

Phase 2—Digging Deeper

Who Reads	Annotations (See page 58.)		
☑ teacher	☐ highlight main points	☐ underline key details	☐ write questions
☑ students	☑ circle key vocabulary	☑ arrows for connections	☐ other: _____

Procedure

1. Review the text, and lead students to describe the structure of this text by asking layered/scaffolded questions:
   - What kind of text is this? Does this text tell a story or give information?
   - Do the things described in this text really happen? How do you know?
   - What do you see in the illustration?
   - Why did the author title this passage *Drip, Drop, Down*?
   - How does the title relate to the text?

2. Reread the text aloud. Ask students, "How does the author use science words to help us understand the water cycle?"

3. Guide students to better understand words such as *evaporates* by using the sentences around the words to help them. Ask students layered/scaffolded questions, such as:
   - When does water evaporate?
   - What causes it?
   - What does the water become?
   - Where does the water go?

4. Annotate using arrows to show connections between the answers to the questions above in other surrounding sentences and the picture and the word *evaporates*.

5. **Partners**—Have partners work together to find and circle other science words that help explain the water cycle. Have partners use the surrounding details to clarify the words.

6. **Whole Class**—Regroup as a class, and display the text for all students. Ask students to share their responses to the meanings of the science words. Annotate the connections between phrases in the text that help the reader understand the circled words.

7. Provide students with copies of the *Water Cycle Word Sort* activity (page 207). Have students work individually or in pairs to sort the words into categories.

8. As a class, use science words from the text to explain the water cycle.

Drip, Drop, Down *(cont.)*

Phase 3—Going Even Deeper

Who Reads	Annotations (See page 58.)

Who Reads
- ☑ teacher
- ☐ students

Annotations (See page 58.)
- ☐ highlight main points
- ☑ circle key vocabulary
- ☑ underline key details
- ☐ arrows for connections
- ☐ write questions
- ☑ other: <u>numbers for sequence</u>

Procedure

1. Review the science words discovered during Phase 2, and tell students that this time when they listen to the passage, they will be more familiar with those scientific words.

2. Read aloud the text to students. Tell students that today, their purpose for listening is to answer the question *How does the author explain the sequence of the water cycle?*

3. **Partners**—After students have listened to the text once, have pairs share their thinking related to the initial question. As needed, ask additional layered/scaffolded questions, such as:
   - What happens first? Next? Then?
   - Why is this order of events important?
   - How does the illustration support the text?

4. **Whole Class**—Regroup as a class, and display the text for all students. Ask students to share their responses to the question regarding how the text describes the water cycle. Annotate the text by writing numbers in the margins to show the sequence of events.

5. Discuss as a class the questions *Why did the author write this text?* and *How do you know?*

Performance Assessment

1. Assign the performance task *Look Up and Down* (page 208).

2. Guide students to think about their work and complete the *Look Up and Down Reflection Page* (page 209).

Drip, Drop, Down

Going Up

1 Imagine a single drop of water. It may be floating in the ocean. Or it could be in a small puddle.

2 As the sun shines, the water gets warm. When it gets warm enough, the droplet evaporates. It becomes water vapor. As a gas, it rises into the sky. There, it is very cold. The water vapor joins other cold droplets. Together, they form a cloud.

Going Down

3 Droplets in the cloud grow heavy and wet. When they are too heavy to stay in the air, they fall. Drip. Drop. Down. Rain and snow fall upon the ground.

4 The water droplet returns to Earth. Slowly, it will trickle down to a lake. Or it may land in a river. In time, it will arrive at the ocean. And the cycle will begin again.

cloud

rain or snow

water vapor

river

ocean

Water Cycle Word Sort

Directions: Read the words in the Word Bank. Sort them into the correct side of the chart.

Up in the Air (Atmosphere)

Down on the Ground

Word Bank

cloud	rain	puddle
ocean	lake	water vapor

Look Up and Down

Directions: Draw what water looks like in the air. Draw what water looks like on the ground. Use the science words you learned to tell about your drawing.

Up in the Air (Atmosphere)	Down on the Ground

Science Words

cloud	rain	puddle
evaporate	lake	water vapor

Note: Students may dictate their words to the teacher.

Look Up and Down Reflection Page

Directions: Think about your work. Did you follow directions?
Circle the *thumbs up* or *thumbs down* picture for each part.

What I Think about My Work

	Yes	No
My drawing for *Up in the Air* is correct.	👍	👎
I used correct science words to tell about my drawing.	👍	👎
My drawing for *Down on the Ground* is correct.	👍	👎
I used correct science words to tell about my drawing.	👍	👎

Teacher comments: _____

_____

_____

_____

_____

Rubric based on work by Lapp, D., B. Moss, M. Grant, & K. Johnson (2015)

How Erasers Work

Purpose

WHAT: Use details from illustrations and words to determine the meaning of a text.

HOW: Apply information from the text to a new situation.

I CAN: I can learn from words and pictures.

Standards

→ **Reading:** Distinguish between information in the picture and in the text.

→ **Writing:** Write explanatory texts.

→ **Language:** Use context clues to determine the meaning of unknown words.

Performance Assessment

→ Students will use information from the passage to explain if crayon can be erased.

Text Selection

→ "How Erasers Work"

→ Text is an informational text organized into paragraphs.

Materials

→ *How Erasers Work* passage, one copy per student (page 216; erasers.pdf)

→ *Look at the Photograph* activity (page 217)

→ *Can Crayon Be Erased?* activity (page 218)

→ *Can Crayon Be Erased? Reflection Page* (page 219)

Text-Dependent Questions (See pages 43–45 for more information.)

→ What is this text about?

→ How does the title help you understand the text?

→ How does the author help you understand the word *abrasive*?

→ How does the photograph help you to understand the text better?

How Erasers Work *(cont.)*

Areas of Complexity

	Measure	Explanation
Quantitative	Lexile Level	520L
Qualitative	Meaning or Purpose	The content of the passage is stated directly. The purpose is to describe how erasers work. Many mechanical processes are described and require visualization to fully comprehend.
	Structure	The structure of the passage is conventional and organized into paragraphs.
	Language Features	The topic of erasers and pencils is known; however, the description of the science behind it includes challenging scientific words and concepts.
Reader/ Task	Knowledge Demands	The text requires students to visualize interactions that cannot be readily seen by the naked eye. Students must understand the technical terms in the text to complete the performance task.

Text Synopsis

Is it magic that erasers make pencil marks disappear? Nope! There is science behind it! This text describes how abrasion makes the eraser rub away the graphite marks made by a pencil in order to make them disappear. But the eraser cannot be too old or dried out. In fact, if the right kind of eraser and writing tool is used, you can even erase ink!

Differentiation

Additional Support—Have students use pencils and erasers to make marks on paper and then erase the marks with different kinds of erasers. Attempt to find an eraser that is old and dried out so that students can see the difficulty with using that kind of eraser.

Extension—Prompt students to identify other places they can see abrasion at work.

How Erasers Work (cont.)

Phase 1—Hitting the Surface

Who Reads	Annotations (See page 58.)		
☑ teacher	☑ highlight main points	☐ underline key details	☑ write questions
☑ students	☑ circle key vocabulary	☐ arrows for connections	☐ other: _____

Procedure

1. Tell students that they will listen to and read a passage several times. Each time will be for a different purpose, to gain a better understanding of the text.

2. Display a copy of the text. Have students follow along as you read the passage aloud. Their goal is to get an overall idea of the text.

3. Ask students, "What is this text about?"

4. After a brief discussion, ask students to follow along and try to understand more about the story as you read the text aloud.

5. **Partners**—After students have listened to you read the passage, ask partners to briefly retell key details and circle any unfamiliar words they would like to understand better.

6. **Whole Class**—Regroup as a class, and display the text for all students. Ask students to share their responses to the initial question. Make annotations on your copy of the text.

7. If needed, ask additional layered/scaffolded questions, such as:
   - What kind of text is this? Does it tell a story or provide information?
   - How does the title help you understand the text?
   - What questions do you have about the text?

8. Have students share any challenging words. Guide them to clarify the words throughout future readings.

Phase 2—Digging Deeper

Who Reads	Annotations (See page 58.)		
☐ teacher	☐ highlight main points	☑ underline key details	☐ write questions
☑ students	☐ circle key vocabulary	☑ arrows for connections	☐ other: _____

How Erasers Work *(cont.)*

Phase 2—Digging Deeper *(cont.)*

Procedure

1. Review with students that they will return to the text to dig deeper into some of the words used in the text. Tell students that they will reread the text, looking for details that may help them understand each word.

2. Display a clean copy of the text. Tell students that, often, the reader can determine what a word means by other details surrounding the unknown vocabulary. Circle the word *abrasion* in the first paragraph. Reread the first paragraph. Ask students to listen to answer the question *How does the author help you understand the word* abrasion?

3. **Partners**—After students have read the first paragraph again, pairs can share their thinking about the meaning of the word *abrasion*. If needed, ask additional layered/scaffolded questions, such as:

   • What does the sentence/words before the word say?
   • What does the sentence/words after the word say?
   • Does what you think the word means make sense?

4. **Whole Class**—Regroup as a class, and display the text for all students. Ask students to share their responses to the question regarding the meaning of the word. Have them support their responses with their annotations. Record annotations on a displayed copy of the text by drawing an arrow between the word *abrasion* and the words in the sentence before *marks go away* and the words in the sentence after *wearing something away*.

5. **Whole Class**—Have students use the challenging words as they explain what they have learned about how erasers work.

Phase 3—Going Even Deeper

Who Reads / Annotations (See page 58.)

☑ teacher   ☐ highlight main points   ☑ underline key details   ☐ write questions

☑ students   ☐ circle key vocabulary   ☑ arrows for connections   ☐ other:_____

Procedure

1. Tell students that they will reread the text, digging deeper to the craft and structure of the passage.

2. Provide students with copies of the *Look at the Photograph* activity (page 217). Have students complete the top half of the page by briefly describing what they see in the photograph.

Phase 3—Going Even Deeper *(cont.)*

Procedure *(cont.)*

3. Display a copy of the text for students to see. Point out that the photographs are the same ones they saw on the activity sheet they just completed. Tell students that the author chooses photographs to go with the text. Sometimes, photographs show details of what the text is about. Other times, the photographs are examples of what the text is about.

4. Tell students that they will reread the text to answer the question *How does the photograph help you to better understand the text?* Encourage students to draw arrows for connections between the text and the photograph and to underline key details that may explain why the photograph was chosen.

5. **Partners**—After students have read and annotated the text once, have pairs share their thinking related to the initial question. If needed, ask layered/scaffolded questions, such as:
   - What does the photograph show?
   - Is what is shown in the photograph described in the text? Where?

6. **Whole Class**—Regroup as a class, and display the text for all students. Ask students to share their responses to the question regarding what the photograph shows. Have them support their responses with their annotations. If possible, record student annotations on a displayed copy of the text.

7. Encourage students to think about whether the photograph clarifies, in visual form, what the text is describing. Do you learn something from the photograph that is not described in the text? Would another photograph show the ideas from the text better?

8. Return to the *Look at the Photograph* activity. Have students complete the bottom part of the page.

Performance Assessment

1. Assign the performance task *Can Crayon Be Erased?* (page 218).

2. Guide students to think about their work and complete the *Can Crayon Be Erased? Reflection Page* (page 219).

How Erasers Work

1   It's almost like magic! You make a mistake in a math problem, and quick as a wink, you erase it and start again. But how do you do it? How exactly do those marks go away? The answer is abrasion. That is the act of wearing something away by friction, or rubbing.

2   Pencil lead is made of graphite. When you use a pencil, bits of graphite attach to the paper. The eraser is abrasive. It must be firm enough to rub and lift the graphite. But it shouldn't be so hard that it wears away the paper.

3   Sometimes, erasers become old and dried out. That makes them too hard and stiff. Try erasing a pencil mark with a dry, old eraser. It will rub across the top of the paper and leave the pencil mark there. Press harder, and it will just tear the paper. An eraser has to be the right kind of hardness to work.

4   Can ink be erased? Sometimes, it can be. But it takes a harder eraser and a different kind of ink. The harder eraser lifts the ink. It also lifts some of the fibers from the paper. The fibers are stained with ink, and the abrasion from the eraser takes them away.

5   Do you need to erase something? It's not magic. It's just abrasion!

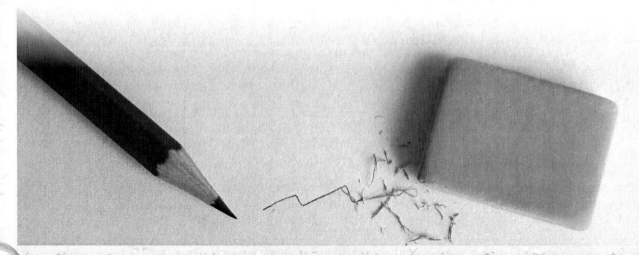

Look at the Photograph

Directions: Look at the photograph. Write about what you see.

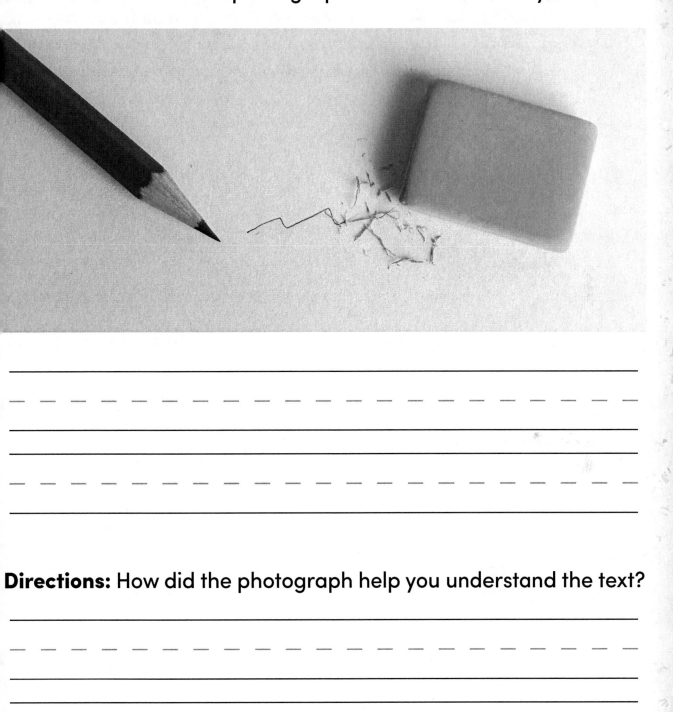

_____

- -

_____

- -

_____

Directions: How did the photograph help you understand the text?

_____

- -

_____

- -

_____

Can Crayon Be Erased?

Directions: Make a crayon mark in the space below. Try to erase it. Did it work? Explain what happened using words from the text.

Crayon Mark

_____

_____

_____

_____

_____

_____

_____

_____

Can Crayon Be Erased? Reflection Page

Directions: Think about your work. Did you follow directions?
Circle the *thumbs up* or *thumbs down* picture for each part.

What I Think about My Work

	Yes	No
I made a crayon mark and tried to erase it.	👍	👎
I said if the crayon mark erased or didn't erase.	👍	👎
I used words from the text to explain why it did/did not erase.	👍	👎

Teacher comments: _____

_____

_____

_____

_____

_____

_____

Rubric based on work by Lapp, D., B. Moss, M. Grant, & K. Johnson (2015)

Bad Breath

Purpose

WHAT: Identify the main purpose of a text.

HOW: Create a poster with the same purpose as the text.

I CAN: I can identify the purpose of a text.

Standards

→ **Reading:** Identify the main purpose of a text.

→ **Writing:** Gather information from a source.

→ **Language:** Determine word meaning using context.

Performance Assessment

→ Students will create dental posters using information from the text.

Text Selection

→ "Bad Breath"

→ Text is informational and organized into paragraphs.

Materials

→ *Bad Breath* passage, one copy per student (page 226; badbreath.pdf)

→ *Knowledge Is Power!* activity (page 227)

→ *Dental Poster* activity (page 228)

→ *Dental Poster Reflection Page* (page 229)

Text-Dependent Questions (See pages 46–48 for more information.)

→ What kind of text is this?

→ What is this text about?

→ What vocabulary tells about bad breath? What do those words mean?

→ Why did the author write this text?

→ What evidence is there for its purpose?

Bad Breath *(cont.)*

Areas of Complexity

	Measure	Explanation
Quantitative	Lexile Level	610L
Qualitative	Meaning or Purpose	The text purpose is to inform the reader of the causes and ways to prevent bad breath.
	Structure	The text is organized into paragraphs. Causes and prevention facts are grouped together within paragraphs. Readers must keep several causes and effects organized in the midst of many details.
	Language Features	The passage opens and closes with informal language. More academic and scientific terms are used in the body.
Reader/ Task	Knowledge Demands	Students must organize and prioritize details to complete the performance task.

Text Synopsis

What is *halitosis*? It's just bad breath. The author tells the reasons for halitosis and how to prevent it. The text encourages readers to take good care of their mouth and teeth.

Differentiation

Additional Support—Read one paragraph at a time with students struggling to understand the text. Ask scaffolded questions until students demonstrate understanding of each paragraph before going on to the next paragraph.

Extension—Have students write about how to prevent stinky feet.

Bad Breath (cont.)

Phase 1—Hitting the Surface

Who Reads	Annotations (See page 59.)		
☑ teacher	☑ highlight main points	☐ underline key details	☐ write questions
☑ students	☑ circle key vocabulary	☐ arrows for connections	☐ other: _____

Procedure

1. Tell students that they will read a text several times. Each time will be for a different purpose, to gain a better understanding of the information.

2. Have students read and annotate the passage to get an overall idea of the text to answer the question *What is this text about?*

3. After students have read and annotated the text once, let them know that you will read the text aloud. Have students follow along and mark the main idea and key details as you read.

4. **Partners**—After students have listened to you read the passage, ask partners to briefly retell the main idea and key details.
   - Does this text give information or tell a story?
   - What does the title say the text is about?
   - What words tell about bad breath?

5. **Whole Class**—Regroup as a class, and display the text for all students. Ask students to share their responses to the question regarding what the text is about. Have them support their responses with their annotations. If possible, record student annotations on a displayed copy of the text.

6. Students should also bring any challenging words to your attention. Guide students to use context clues to clarify key words throughout subsequent readings.

Phase 2—Digging Deeper

Who Reads	Annotations (See page 59.)		
☐ teacher	☐ highlight main points	☑ underline key details	☐ write questions
☑ students	☑ circle key vocabulary	☐ arrows for connections	☐ other: _____

Phase 2—Digging Deeper *(cont.)*

Procedure

1. Review with students that rereading a text for a different purpose is one way to more fully understand the text. Tell students that they will reread the text to identify vocabulary that will help them comprehend the text better. They will read to answer the questions *What vocabulary tells about bad breath?* and *What do those words mean?*

2. Have students reread the text in search of words that tell about bad breath. Have students circle key vocabulary and draw arrows to surrounding words that help them understand the key vocabulary. Ask students layered/scaffolded questions as needed, such as:
   - What part of speech is the word? How can you tell?
   - How does the text around the word help you understand the word?
   - Does what you think the word means make sense in the sentence?

3. If needed, model clarifying words with the following example:
   - Reread the first paragraph to students. Annotate by circling the word *foul* and say, "I am going to circle the word *foul* because I am not sure what that word means."
   - Tell students that the meaning of unknown words can be figured out by the context or words and ideas surrounding the text.
   - Tell students, "I read about stinky feet and passed gas right before the word *foul*. I read about an unpleasant smell in the sentence right after. I think the word means 'stinky.'"
   - Test the word *stinky* in the sentence in place of the word *foul* to show students that it does make sense.
   - Annotate the text by drawing arrows from the word *foul* to context clues that helped you figure out the meaning of *foul*.

4. **Partners**—After students have read and annotated the text, have pairs share with each other the words they circled.

5. **Whole Class**—Regroup as a class, and display the text for all students. Ask students to share the words they circled. Annotate the words on a displayed copy of the text. Create a poster to list the words students identify as relating to bad breath.

Phase 3—Going Even Deeper

Who Reads	Annotations (See page 59.)		
☐ teacher	☐ highlight main points	☑ underline key details	☐ write questions
☑ students	☑ circle key vocabulary	☐ arrows for connections	☐ other: _____

Phase 3—Going Even Deeper *(cont.)*

Procedure

1. Encourage students that each time they read a text for a different purpose, they are digging deeper and better understanding the text.

2. Review and identify the various reasons authors write texts. Create a poster or display with the three main purposes: entertain, persuade, and inform. Discuss each briefly, including providing examples for each that students will be familiar with.

3. Tell students that they will reread the text to answer the questions *Why did the author write this text?* and *What evidence is there for its purpose?* Have students annotate the text by underlining key details to show where there is evidence for the purpose of the text.

4. **Partners**—After students have read and annotated the text, have pairs share their thinking related to the question of the author's purpose. If needed, ask layered/scaffolded questions, such as:
   - Did the author convince you to do something? What parts of the text convinced you?
   - Did you learn something by reading this text? What parts of the text taught you?
   - Did the text move you emotionally—make you laugh/cry/happy/sad? What parts of the text moved you?

5. **Whole Class**—Regroup as a class, and display the text for all students. Ask students to share their responses to the question regarding the author's purpose. Have them support their responses with their annotations. If possible, record student annotations on a displayed copy of the text.

6. Discuss with students that sometimes texts have multiple purposes. Help students identify the purpose of this text. Students may say it is to inform the reader about causes and prevention of halitosis. Students may say it is to persuade the reader to prevent halitosis. Or students may say that the purpose is to entertain because the first paragraph is funny. Guide students to identify sentences that support their responses. You may wish to highlight the sentences by color coding them according to their purposes. Have a discussion about which purpose the text had most sentences about.

7. Provide students with *Knowledge Is Power!* (page 227). Have students work individually or with partners to identify causes and preventions for halitosis.

Performance Assessment

1. Assign the performance task *Dental Poster* (page 228).

2. Guide students to think about their work and complete the *Dental Poster Reflection Page* (page 229).

Bad Breath

1 Let's face it. People don't always smell so good. From stinky feet to passed gas, there are many ways that people project some foul body odors. Halitosis is one unpleasant way to smell! But the good news is that it is very easy to prevent.

2 What is halitosis? It's just plain old bad breath, and it's mainly caused by not brushing your teeth very well. Bacteria that cause odors can grow in your mouth. They grow on bits of food left in your mouth or stuck between your teeth. There is a simple solution for that! Brush your teeth thoroughly.

3 Many people just brush for a few seconds. It is important to brush your teeth for at least two minutes twice a day. Use dental floss as well. And don't forget to brush your tongue! Food and bacteria can linger there, too.

4 Foods with intense odors, such as garlic and onions, are another cause of bad breath. They have strong-smelling oils that filter to your lungs and then come out your mouth. Those smells go away after a while, though.

5 One big cause of bad breath is very easy to prevent. It is smoking. If you don't smoke, you will never have smoker's breath!

6 Take good care of your mouth and teeth every day. Then, people will be able to see you coming before they smell you!

Knowledge Is Power!

Directions: Read paragraphs 2–4. List the causes of halitosis in the top of the chart. List the ways to prevent halitosis in the bottom of the chart.

Causes of Halitosis

Prevention of Halitosis

Dental Poster

Directions: Make a poster for a dentist's office. Show how halitosis is caused. Show how halitosis can be prevented. Use details from the text.

Dental Poster Reflection Page

Directions: Think about your work. Write a check mark in the *Yes* or *No* column to show if you did all parts of the project.

What I Think about My Work

	Yes	No
My poster tells what halitosis is.		
My poster tells how to prevent halitosis.		
My poster includes information from "Bad Breath."		
My poster is neat and easy to understand.		

Teacher comments: _____

_____

_____

_____

_____

Rubric based on work by Lapp, D., B. Moss, M. Grant, & K. Johnson (2015)

Too Cold for Trees!

Purpose

WHAT: Connect details from illustrations and words to determine meaning.

HOW: Draw and dictate sentences about a tundra animal.

I CAN: I can learn information from words and pictures.

Standards

→ **Reading:** With prompting and support, describe the relationship between the illustrations and the text.

→ **Writing:** Use a combination of drawing, dictating, and writing to compose informative text to name and supply information about the topic.

→ **Language:** Use words and phrases acquired through conversations, reading and being read to, and responding to texts.

→ **Science:** Use a model to represent the relationship between the needs of different plants or animals (including humans) and the places they live.

Performance Assessment

→ With prompting and support from the teacher, students will draw a picture of the tundra and use important words and information from "Too Cold for Trees!" to dictate three sentences that support the illustrations.

Text Selection

→ "Too Cold for Trees!"

→ Text is chunked into paragraphs. It includes many connected facts.

Materials

→ *Too Cold for Trees!* passage, one copy per student (page 236; toocold.pdf)

→ *What Is the Tundra Like?* activity (page 237)

→ *My Tundra Animal* activity (page238)

→ *My Tundra Animal Reflection Page* (page 239)

Text-Dependent Questions (See pages 40–42 for more information.)

→ What is the author telling us? What is the artist showing us?

→ What does the author do to help you understand the science word *biome*?

→ Why is it hard to live in this biome?

→ Why did the author title the text "Too Cold for Trees!"?

→ How do the animals survive?

Too Cold for Trees! *(cont.)*

Areas of Complexity

Measure		Explanation
Quantitative	Lexile Level	210L
Qualitative	Meaning or Purpose	The content is presented in a formal, scientific way. The purpose is to describe the plants and animals of the tundra.
	Structure	The structure of the passage is academic, informational text.
	Language Features	The language is challenging and specific to the topic.
Reader/ Task	Knowledge Demands	The text requires understanding of the concept of biomes, the variety of life on Earth, and a general comprehension of the structure of the world. Students must integrate details from the text and images to complete the performance task.

Text Synopsis

This informational text presents facts about the tundra. It describes the plants and animals that live there and what special features allow those living things to survive the harsh environment.

Differentiation

Additional Support—Ask scaffolded questions that build to the intended understanding that it is difficult for animals and plants to survive in the tundra.

If additional scaffolds are needed, present items or photographs related to the text (e.g., fur, ice, or white things) to make the important words more concrete.

As needed, help students to restate their responses using the new words from the text.

Extension—Prompt students to compare the tundra to their environments. Have students imagine what they would need to survive in the tundra.

Too Cold for Trees! (cont.)

Phase 1—Hitting the Surface

Who Reads

☑ teacher

☐ students

Annotations (See page 58.)

☐ highlight main points ☐ underline key details ☐ write questions

☐ circle key vocabulary ☐ arrows for connections ☐ other: _____

Procedure

1. Tell students that they will listen to a text several times. Each time will be for a different purpose, to gain a better understanding of the text.

2. Display a copy of the text. Have students listen to you read the passage to get an overall idea of the passage.

3. Ask students, "What is this passage about?"

4. **Partners**—After students have listened to you read the text once, ask partners to share what they think the text is about.

5. **Whole Class**—Regroup as a class, and display the text for all students. Ask students to share their responses to the initial question. Make annotations on your copy of the text.

Phase 2—Digging Deeper

Who Reads

☑ teacher

☑ students

Annotations (See page 58.)

☐ highlight main points ☑ underline key details ☐ write questions

☑ circle key vocabulary ☐ arrows for connections ☑ other: <u>write question marks</u>

Procedure

1. Before returning the text, say, "Let's read the passage again. This time, pay close attention to the words to get more information about the tundra."

2. **Partners**—Form student pairs. Ask students to talk to their partners about the text-dependent question *What is the author telling us about?*

3. **Whole Class**—Call on students to share their thoughts about the text-dependent question *What is the author telling us about?* Encourage students to point to parts of the text or images as they respond.

4. Ask students to look at the displayed text to answer the question *What is the atrist showing us?*

Too Cold for Trees! *(cont.)*

Phase 2—Digging Deeper *(cont.)*

Procedure *(cont.)*

5. Before returning to the text, say, "We are going to return to 'Too Cold for Trees!' This time, think about the question *How does the author help you understand the science word* biome? We do not hear science words very often. We use them to talk about science topics like places on Earth or parts of animals and plants."

6. Direct students to listen for the science word *biome* as you read. Students should raise their hands when they hear it, then guide you (or a student volunteer) to find and circle it on the displayed text.

7. Model using context clues and your own prior knowledge to define *biomes*. Underline details (text or image) that help define the word, and write a short definition or draw a picture to represent the word in the margin on the projected copy for everyone to see.

   • You may choose to repeat this process with the science words *tundra* and *hibernate*.

8. Before returning to the text, say, "Now that we understand more of the words in the text, let's reread to get more details about the tundra. Think about the question *Why is it hard to live in this biome?*

9. If needed, stop frequently to ask students if they heard details that address the question. Highlight the text that corresponds to their responses. If needed, ask additional questions, such as:

   • What would make it hard to live there?
   • How do the animals survive?

10. Read the caption that accompanies the photograph. Ask students to describe what they see. Guide them to use the photograph to answer the question *Why is it hard to live in this biome?* If needed, ask additional questions, such as:

   • What color are the animals in the picture?
   • Look at the plants in the picture. Are they tall or short? Do they have a lot of leaves?
   • What is in the photograph that is behind the words?

Phase 3—Going Even Deeper

Who Reads	Annotations (See page 58.)		
☑ teacher	☑ highlight main points	☐ underline key details	☐ write questions
☑ students	☐ circle key vocabulary	☑ arrows for connections	☐ other: _____

Phase 3—Going Even Deeper *(cont.)*

Procedure

1. Remind students that readers often need to read or listen to a text more than once. During each reading, they think about different things.

2. Before returning to the text, say, "Let's read the text in two parts. We will read the first half, paying close attention to the words and photograph that give us information about plants."

3. Read the first two paragraphs aloud. Direct students to raise their hands when you read information about plants or trees. Guide students to highlight plant-related words on your displayed copy of the passage or on individual copies of the passage.

4. After highlighting plant information, ask students if there is anything in the photograph that matches or tells more. Draw arrows to connect the text to the photograph. Monitor student responses to help you identify students who may be struggling with the concept.

5. **Partners**—Have partners talk about the plant-related words and plant pictures in the text. Ask, "Why did the author title the text 'Too Cold for Trees!'?"

6. Say, "Now, we will read the second half of the text, paying close attention to the words and photograph that give us information about animals."

7. Read the last two paragraphs aloud. Have students raise their hands when you read information about animals. Invite students to highlight animal-related words on your displayed copy of the passage or on individual copies of the passage.

8. After highlighting animal-related words, ask students if there is anything in the photograph that matches or tells more. Draw arrows to connect the text to the photograph. Monitor student responses to help you identify students who may be struggling with the concept.

9. **Partners**—Have partners talk about the animal-related words and animal photograph in the text.

10. **Whole Class**—Regroup as a class, and display the text for all students. Ask students to use plant-related words and photos and the animal-related words and photos to describe the tundra.

11. Have students complete the *What Is the Tundra Like?* activity (page 237). Have them refer back to the text and photograph as they work. If needed, call the group back together to revisit the text with teacher guidance.

Performance Assessment

1. Assign the performance task *My Tundra Animal* (page 238).

2. Guide students to think about their work and complete the *My Tundra Animal Reflection Page* (page 239).

Too Cold for Trees!

1 There are many biomes on Earth. The tundra is the coldest. Very little can survive there.

2 Temperatures often drop below zero in the tundra. The air is very dry. There are no trees. It is too cold. Only short, dry plants can grow there.

3 Some tundra animals have white fur. They blend in with the snow. In the winter, some animals hide from the cold. They hibernate. They sleep for months. Others slowly move south.

4 The tundra is a harsh place. Only the strongest survive there.

polar bears

What Is the Tundra Like?

Directions: Listen to each question. Circle the words that tell about the tundra.

Questions	Words	
Is the tundra hot or cold?	hot	cold
Is the tundra wet or dry?	wet	dry
Are plants in the tundra tall or short?	tall	short
Are most animals in the tundra white or colorful?	white	colorful
Are things that live in the tundra weak or strong?	weak	strong

My Tundra Animal

Directions: Create your own tundra animal. Draw, write, and speak about your animal. Use science words from the text.

Word Bank			
cold	tundra	biome	dry
harsh	hibernate	temperature	survive

_____

1. My animal is _____ .

2. It can live in the tundra because

_____

_____ .

Name: _____ Date: _____

My Tundra Animal Reflection Page

Directions: Think about your work. Did you follow directions? Circle the *thumbs up* or *thumbs down* picture for each part.

What I Think about My Work

	Yes	No
My picture has details.	👍	👎
My sentences describe why my animal can live in the tundra.	👍	👎
My picture matches my words.	👍	👎
I used science words from the text.	👍	👎

Teacher comments: _____

_____

_____

_____

_____

Rubric based on work by Lapp, D., B. Moss, M. Grant, & K. Johnson (2015)

Dear Mayor Keen and Dog Behavior

Purpose

WHAT: Identify reasons that support a main idea across two texts.

HOW: Draw a dog park using details from two texts.

I CAN: I can use details from two texts.

Standards

→ **Reading:** Identify reasons an author gives to support an idea.

→ **Reading:** Identify similarities and differences between two texts.

→ **Writing:** Draw and label a picture, and write a sentence in response to a prompt.

→ **Language:** Identify and use verbs.

Performance Assessment

→ Students will draw and label a picture of a dog park. They will write sentences telling how the dogs will feel while at the dog park.

Text Selection

→ "Dear Mayor Keen"

→ "Dog Behavior"

→ "Dear Mayor Keen" is written as a letter.

→ "Dog Behavior" is written in paragraph format.

Materials

→ *Dear Mayor Keen* and *Dog Behavior* passages, one copy per student (page 246; mayorkeendogbehavior.pdf)

→ *How Dogs Act* activity (page 247)

→ *A Dog Park* activity (page 248)

→ *A Dog Park Reflection Page* (page 249)

Text-Dependent Questions (See pages 43–45 for more information.)

→ What is this text about?

→ What kind of text is this?

→ What are the reasons for the boy's request?

Dear Mayor Keen and Dog Behavior

Areas of Complexity

	Measure	Explanation
Quantitative	Lexile Level	"Dear Mayor Keen"—490L "Dog Behavior"—240L
Qualitative	Meaning or Purpose	"Dear Mayor Keen"—Oscar writes this letter to make a request to the mayor for the city to open a dog park. The limitations of traditional parks and the negative effect on dogs are implied. "Dog Behavior"—This text was written to describe how young dogs behave.
Qualitative	Structure	"Dear Mayor Keen"—This text is written in letter format. It opens with a request and is followed by reasons. "Dog Behavior"—This text is in paragraph form, composed of simple and compound sentences.
Qualitative	Language Features	Vocabulary used to describe animal behavior is used in both texts.
Reader/ Task	Knowledge Demands	Readers benefit from knowing that the letter is written to the mayor because a city provides park services. Students must compare character information to nonfiction information to integrate both texts. Students must integrate details from the texts to complete the performance task.

Text Synopsis

"Dear Mayor Keen"—Oscar Trent and his dog, Spot, write a letter to Mayor Keen, asking for the city to open a dog park. Oscar describes his dog's need for a dog park based on what the dog is not able to do (run freely) and based on what his dog would do if there were a dog park (race and scamper). Oscar closes his letter by asking the mayor to respond with his thoughts on the matter.

"Dog Behavior"—This paragraph describes the playful behavior of young dogs.

Differentiation

Additional Support—If needed, provide the visual aid of a video or photograph for students who may not know how a dog park is different from a traditional park. Discuss the difference between dogs being walked on a leash and being able to play freely.

Extension—Have students write letters to the mayor about a place for kittens to play. Students should include their rationale for having such a place and what it should look like. How would it be different from a dog park? How would it meet the unique needs of kittens?

Phase 1—Hitting the Surface

Who Reads

☑ teacher

☐ students

Annotations (See page 58.)

☑ highlight main points   ☐ underline key details   ☐ write questions

☑ circle key vocabulary   ☐ arrows for connections   ☐ other: _____

Procedure

1. Tell students that they will listen to and read a passage several times. Each time will be for a different purpose, to gain a better understanding of the text.

2. Display a copy of "Dear Mayor Keen" (page 246). Have students follow along as you read the passage aloud. Their goal is to get an overall idea of the text.

3. Ask students, "What is this text about?"

4. After a brief discussion, ask students to follow along and try to understand more about the story as you reread the text aloud.

5. **Partners**—After students have listened to you read the passage, ask partners to briefly retell key details and circle any unfamiliar words they would like to better understand.

6. **Whole Class**—Regroup as a class, and display the text for all students. Ask students to share their responses to the initial question. Make annotations on your copy of the text.

7. If needed, ask additional layered/scaffolded questions, such as:
   - To whom is this letter written?
   - Who is the letter from?
   - What is this letter about?
   - Why was the letter written?
   - Who does Oscar describe in the letter?

8. Display a copy of "Dog Behavior." Have students listen to you read the passage to get an overall idea of the text.

9. Ask students, "What is this text about?"

10. **Partners**—After students have listened to you read the text once, ask partners to briefly retell key details.

11. **Whole Class**—Regroup as a class, and display the text for all students. Ask students to share their responses to the initial question. Make annotations on your copy of the text.

12. Have students share any words that are challenging. Guide them to clarify the words throughout future readings.

Dear Mayor Keen and Dog Behavior *(cont.)*

Phase 2—Digging Deeper

Who Reads	Annotations (See page 58.)		
☐ teacher	☐ highlight main points	☑ underline key details	☐ write questions
☑ students	☐ circle key vocabulary	☐ arrows for connections	☐ other: _____

Procedure

1. Review with students that they identified *what* Oscar Trent wants in his letter to the mayor in their first reading of the text. Tell students that they will reread the text for the purpose of identifying the reasons Oscar lists for wanting a dog park built in the city.

2. Ask students to reread the text. Students should underline key details as they answer the question *What are the reasons for the boy's request?*

3. Partners—After students have read and annotated the text once, have pairs share their thinking related to the initial question. Support students by asking layered/scaffolded questions, such as:

  · What does Oscar's dog do during the day? At night?
  · How do dogs act when they are happy?
  · Is Oscar's dog happy or sad? How do you know?
  · How would a dog park help?

4. Whole Class—Regroup as a class, and display the text for all students. Ask students to share their responses to the question regarding what the text is about. Have them support their responses with their annotations. If possible, record student annotations on a displayed copy of the text.

5. Provide students with the *How Dogs Act* activity (page 247). Have students work individually or with partners to use evidence from the text to complete the table. Ask students to look for *verbs* that show how dogs behave to help them locate words to complete the chart.

Phase 3—Going Even Deeper

Who Reads	Annotations (See page 58.)		
☐ teacher	☐ highlight main points	☑ underline key details	☐ write questions
☑ students	☐ circle key vocabulary	☐ arrows for connections	☐ other:_____

Procedure

1. Tell students that they will read "Dog Behavior" and compare it to "Dear Mayor Keen." Explain that they will first read "Dog Behavior" to find out what it is about. As they read the text, have them annotate the text by underlining key details they learn about puppies to answer the question *What is this text about?*

2. **Whole Class**—Regroup as a class, and display the text for all students. Ask students to share their responses to the question regarding what the text is about. Have them support their responses with their annotations. If possible, record student annotations on a displayed copy of the text.

3. Return to the text "Dear Mayor Keen" and the chart created during Phase 2. Ask students to compare and contrast the two texts. Begin with a general discussion of the two texts by asking:
   - What is the format of the first text?
   - What is the format of the second text?

4. **Whole Class**—Tell students that since both texts describe the behavior of dogs, they can compare and contrast the information about Spot and the information about dogs in general to see what the texts say is the same and what is different. Tell students that they will do this to answer the questions:
   - How is the dog in the letter the same as the dogs described in the paragraph?
   - How is the dog in the letter different than the dogs describe in the paragraph?

5. Create a Venn diagram on a piece of chart paper. Label one circle *Spot* and the other circle *Dogs*. Label the overlapping section *Both*. Work with students to read "Dog Behavior" and compare the behavior to dogs in "Dear Mayor Keen." Have students complete the Venn diagram using evidence from both texts.

6. Have students use the Venn diagram to orally create sentences to describe the behavior of just dogs, just kittens, or both dogs and kittens. For example, "Both dogs and kittens run. Only kittens pretend to hunt."

Performance Assessment

1. Assign the performance task *A Dog Park* (page 248).

2. Guide students to think about their work and complete the *A Dog Park Reflection Page* (page 249).

Dear Mayor Keen

1 Dear Mayor Keen,

2 I am writing to ask the city to open a dog park. During the day, my dog stays in the house. At night, we take walks. But we always need to keep him on a leash. There are no places for him to run freely. This makes me sad. Dogs are happiest when they can scamper and play fetch. They love to race each other. I know my dog misses jogging in the grass. His tail barely wags. If we had a park with a fence, the dogs here could run and play. They would be healthier and happier.

3 Please let me know what you think!

4 Sincerely,

5 Oscar Trent and Spot

Dog Behavior

1 Dogs like to play. They chase balls and toys.

2 They pretend to hunt. They wrestle with each other.

3 Puppies jump, run, and pounce when they play.

4 Sometimes, they get rough. But when they are done, they cuddle.

How Dogs Act

Directions: Think about how Spot acts without a dog park. How would he act if he had a dog park to go to? Write or draw your ideas below.

Spot with a Dog Park

Spot without a Dog Park

A Dog Park

Directions: What should a dog park look like? Draw a picture. Label it with two details from the texts. Write a sentence about how the dogs will feel.

```



```

_____

_____

_____

A Dog Park Reflection Page

Directions: Think about your work. Did you follow directions?
Circle the *thumbs up* or *thumbs down* picture for each part.

What I Think about My Work

	Yes	No
My drawing is a picture of a dog park.	👍	👎
I included two details from the text.	👍	👎
I labeled my drawing.	👍	👎
I wrote a sentence that tells how the dogs will feel.	👍	👎

Teacher comments: _____

_____

_____

_____

_____

Rubric based on work by Lapp, D., B. Moss, M. Grant, & K. Johnson (2015)

Playing It Safe and My Story

Purpose

WHAT: Combine details from an informational text and a narrative text.

HOW: Write letters using information from two texts.

I CAN: I can use information from two texts.

Standards

→ **Reading:** Compare and contrast points presented by two texts on the same topic.

→ **Writing:** Write to inform using facts.

→ **Language:** Recognize formal and informal language.

Performance Assessment

→ Students will write letters to a character from the text using information from another text.

Text Selection

→ "Playing It Safe"

→ "My Story"

→ "Playing It Safe" is an informational text chunked into paragraphs.

→ "My Story" is a narrative text chunked into paragraphs.

Materials

→ *Playing It Safe* and *My Story* passages, one copy per student (page 256; playingsafemystory.pdf)

→ *Playing Safely* activity (page 257)

→ *Dear Hurt Player* activity (page 258)

→ *Dear Hurt Player Reflection Page* (page 259)

Text-Dependent Questions (See pages 46–48 for more information.)

→ What is the text about?

→ What kind of text is this?

→ What is the focus of each paragraph?

→ How are the two texts connected?

→ What did you learn in "Playing It Safe" that can help you understand why the soccer player got hurt in "My Story"?

Playing It Safe and My Story *(cont.)*

Areas of Complexity

	Measure	Explanation
Quantitative	Lexile Level	"Playing It Safe"—380L "My Story"—330L
Qualitative	Meaning or Purpose	"Playing It Safe"—The text informs the reader of ways to stay safe when playing sports. "My Story"—The text is a narrative about what happened when a soccer player got hurt.
	Structure	"Playing It Safe"—The passage follows a main idea, supporting detail, and example structure. "My Story"—The story is told out of sequence, beginning with an injury, followed by the events leading up to being hurt.
	Language Features	Vocabulary that is specific to the topic of sports is used in both texts. The point of view and voice in the texts are different while the content is related.
Reader/Task	Knowledge Demands	Students must keep the details of two different texts in mind in order to compare and contrast information in them. The ideas must be integrated to complete the performance task.

Text Synopsis

"Playing It Safe"—Playing sports is fun, but getting hurt isn't! This informational text explains ways to stay safe by using protective gear and warming up. Examples of each are provided.

"My Story"—Getting hurt is not fun, but that is what has happened to a boy playing soccer. Events after the injury are described, such as not being able to move, getting the coach's assistance, and icing the leg. The text ends with the player wishing he would have warmed up before the game.

Differentiation

Additional Support—Help students understand what it means to warm up by having them practice warming up. Follow the suggestions in "Playing It Safe." Discuss how stretching and jogging help warm up the muscles.

Extension—Have students list additional protective gear they use in the chart created in Phase 2. Another option would be to have students write about a time they got hurt and what they could have done to prevent it.

Phase 1—Hitting the Surface

Who Reads	Annotations (See page 59.)		
☑ teacher	☑ highlight main points	☐ underline key details	☐ write questions
☑ students	☑ circle key vocabulary	☐ arrows for connections	☐ other: _____

Procedure

1. Tell students that they will read a text several times. Each time will be for a different purpose, to gain a better understanding of the information.

2. Have students read and annotate "Playing It Safe" to get an overall idea of the text to answer the question *What is this text about?*

3. After students have read and annotated the text once, let them know you will read the text aloud. Have students follow along and mark the main idea and key details as you read.

4. **Partners**—After students have listened to you read the story, ask partners to briefly retell the main idea and key details. Be sure they reference the text in each response.
   - Does this text tell a story or give information?
   - What kind of information does the text give?
   - How is the text organized?

5. **Whole Class**—Regroup as a class, and display the text for all students. Ask students to share their responses to the question regarding what the text is about. Have them support their responses with their annotations. If possible, record student annotations on a displayed copy of the text.

6. Have students read "My Story" (page 256) to get an overall idea of the passage to answer the question *What is this text about?*

7. After students have read and annotated the text once, let them know you will read the text aloud. Have students follow along and mark the main idea and key details as you read.

8. **Partners**—After students have listened to you read the story, ask partners to briefly retell the main idea and key details.

Playing It Safe and My Story *(cont.)*

Phase 2—Digging Deeper

Who Reads	Annotations (See page 59.)

Who Reads

☑ teacher

☑ students

Annotations (See page 59.)

❑ highlight main points   ☑ underline key details   ❑ write questions

☑ circle key vocabulary   ❑ arrows for connections   ❑ other: _____

Procedure

1. Review with students that they will read the text for multiple purposes. Explain that, this time, they will read to identify how the text is organized and to answer the question *What is the focus of each paragraph?*

2. Have students read the second paragraph to answer the question *What is the focus of the paragraph?* Encourage students to annotate their copies of the text as they read.

3. If needed, model annotating the main idea and key details.
   - Read aloud the first paragraph to students. Say, "I see in the first sentence that it is good to play sports. This whole text is about playing sports. I am going to underline *play sports*. The sentence goes on to say it is *not good to get hurt*. This idea is connected to the title of playing safe. I am going to draw an arrow from the words *not good to get hurt* back to the title 'Playing It Safe.'"
   - Continue to read and identify that the second sentence is about staying safe by wearing protective gear.
   - Circle key vocabulary in the following sentences that tell more about protective gear (helmets, elbow pads, and kneepads).
   - Have students annotate the rest of the text individually or on the displayed copy.

4. **Partners**—After students have read and annotated the text once, pairs can share their thinking as related to the initial question. If needed, ask additional layered/scaffolded questions, such as:
   - What does the first sentence of the paragraph say?
   - How can injury be prevented?
   - What happens if injury does happen?

5. **Whole Class**—Create a two-column chart. Title the top left of the chart *Protective Gear*. Title the top right of the chart *Warm Up*. Have students use the annotations they made in the text to help fill the chart with details that support each main idea.

Phase 3—Going Even Deeper

Who Reads	Annotations (See page 59.)		
☐ teacher	☑ highlight main points	☐ underline key details	☐ write questions
☑ students	☑ circle key vocabulary	☐ arrows for connections	☐ other:_____

Procedure

1. Tell students that they will read a second text called "My Story." Provide students with the text, and allow them to preview the title and photograph. Ask students to read through the text to get an overall understanding of the text. They should read to answer the questions *What kind of text is this?* and *What is this text about?* Encourage students to annotate the text as they read by highlighting main points and circling key vocabulary.

2. **Whole Class**—Regroup as a class, and display the text for all students. Ask students to share their responses to the question regarding what the text is about. Have them support their responses with their annotations. If possible, record student annotations on a displayed copy of the text.

3. **Partners**—Have partners discuss their answers to the question about how the two texts are connected.

4. **Whole Class**—Regroup as a class, and display the text for all students. Ask students to share their responses to the question regarding how the two texts are connected. Have them support their responses with their annotations. If possible, record student annotations on a displayed copy of the text. Students should have a strong understanding that "Playing It Safe" is an informational text about many ways to stay safe while playing sports, and "My Story" is a narrative text that tells about a child who gets hurt playing sports.

5. Refer back to "Playing It Safe." Ask students to reread each text to answer the question *How are the two texts connected?* Have students refer back to the answers to the questions *What kind of text is this?* and *What is this text about?*

6. Strengthen students' understanding of "My Story" by having them use what they know about both texts to complete the *Playing Safely* activity (page 257). Students can complete this activity independently or in pairs to answer the question *What did you learn in "Playing It Safe" that can help you understand why the soccer player got hurt in "My Story"?*

Performance Assessment

1. Assign the performance task *Dear Hurt Player* (page 258).

2. Guide students to think about their work and complete the *Dear Hurt Player Reflection Page* (page 259).

Playing It Safe

1   It's good to play sports, but it's not good to get hurt. To stay safe, remember to wear protective gear. Helmets are a good idea. Elbow pads and kneepads also help. Make sure you use the right kind of gear for your sport.

2   Remember to warm up. Jog a little bit, and then do some stretching. Warm muscles won't get hurt as easily. If you get injured, stop and rest. If the pain continues, hold an ice pack where you got injured. If you are hurt very badly, you may need to see a doctor.

My Story

1   Today, I got hurt! It wasn't awful, but it really hurt. I was playing soccer. I pulled a muscle. I couldn't move. When the coach came over, I told him that I hurt my leg.

2   He helped me off the field. I felt like crying, but I hid my tears. Someone ran to get the team's first-aid supplies. Someone else got ice. I guess I should have warmed up before the game.

Playing Safely

Directions: List the safety ideas from the two texts.

Protective Gear

Warm Up

Dear Hurt Player

Directions: Write a letter to the hurt player in "My Story." Tell him what he should do next time to prevent an injury. Use information from "Playing It Safe" to help you.

Dear _____,

_____

_____

_____

_____

_____

_____

_____

Sincerely,

_____

Dear Hurt Player Reflection Page

Directions: Think about your work. Write a check mark in the *Yes* or *No* column to show if you did all of the parts of the project.

What I Think about My Work

	Yes	No
My letter tells how the player can prevent an injury.		
My letter uses information from "Playing It Safe."		
My letter is written in letter format.		

Teacher comments: _____

_____

_____

_____

_____

Rubric based on work by Lapp, D., B. Moss, M. Grant, & K. Johnson (2015)

Try It!

Use the passage and the planning forms that follow to plan a close reading lesson.

Hang Ten, Dude (Lexile 460L)

Surfing began thousands of years ago. The first boards were made of wood. They were big and heavy. Later, they were made of foam. Over time, boards became smaller. Today, surfboards are very sleek. And they often have fancy fins to help surfers steer.

Some of the first surfers may have been fishers. Historians think they rode waves to carry home the fish they caught. What is clear is that surfing soon grew to be a sport. It was a way to compete and have fun. Today, people surf around the world. Surfers say nothing beats being out on the water. They love being in the sun. But they also love the challenge. They try over and over to catch the perfect wave. And now, more people are trying the sport than ever before.

Planning Chart for Close Reading

Planning

Date:_____ Grade: _____ Discipline:_____

Purpose(s): _____

Standard(s):_____

Text Selection (literary or informational):_____

Performance Assessment: _____

Materials: _____

Text Selection

Title: _____

Author: _____

Page(s) or Section(s): _____

How should this text be chunked? _____

_____

Areas of Complexity

Lexile Level:_____

Meaning or Purpose:_____

Structure: _____

Language Features:_____

Knowledge Demands: _____

Text-Dependent Questions

1. _____

2. _____

3. _____

4. _____

5. _____

Performance Task

_____

_____

_____

_____

Differentiation

Additional Support: _____

_____

Extension:_____

_____

Try It! (cont.)

Teaching Close Reading

Teaching

Limited Frontloading ❑ yes ❑ no

Describe:

First Read

Who Reads? ❑ teacher ❑ student

Student Materials

❑ graphic organizer   ❑ group consensus form

❑ note taking guide   ❑ summary form

Second Read

Who Reads? ❑ teacher ❑ student

Student Materials

❑ graphic organizer   ❑ group consensus form

❑ note taking guide   ❑ summary form

Additional Reads

Who Reads? ❑ teacher ❑ student

Student Resources

❑ graphic organizer   ❑ group consensus form

❑ note taking guide   ❑ summary form

Extension	Reteaching

ACT. 2006. "Reading Between the Lines: What the ACT Reveals About College Readiness in Reading." https://www.act.org/research/policymakers/pdf/reading_report.pdf.

Airasian, Peter W., Kathleen A. Cruikshank, Richard E. Mayer, Paul R. Pintrich, James Raths, and Merlin C. Wittrock. 2001. *A Taxonomy for Learning, Teaching, and Assessing: A Revision of Bloom's Taxonomy of Educational Objectives (Complete edition)*. Edited by Lorin W. Anderson and David R. Krathwohl. New York: Longman.

Boyles, Nancy. 2012. "Closing in on Close Reading." *Educational Leadership (Association for Supervision and Curriculum Development)* 70 (4): 36–41.

Coleman, David, and Susan Pimentel. 2012. *Revised Publishers' Criteria for the Common Core State Standards in English Language Arts and Literacy, Grades 3–12*.

Common Core State Initiative. 2012. *Common Core State Standards for English Language Arts, Appendix A (Additional Information)*. NGA and CCSSO.

Fountas, Sue, and Gay Pinnell. 2012. "F&P Text Level Gradient." *Heinemann*. http://www.heinemann.com/fountasandpinnell/handouts/FP_TextLevelGradient.pdf.

_____. 2015. "Instructional Grade-Level Equivalence Chart." http://www.fountasandpinnell.com/shared/resources/FP_FPL_Chart_Instructional-Grade-Level-Equivalence-Chart.pdf

Lapp, Diane, Barbara Moss, Maria Grant, and Kelly Johnson. 2015. "A Close Look at Close Reading: Teaching Students to Analyze Complex Texts, Grades K–5." ASCD.

National Governors Association Center for Best Practices & Council of Chief State School Officers. 2010. *Common Core State Standards for English Language Arts and Literacy in History/Social Studies, Science, and Technical Subjects*. Washington, DC: Authors.

Partnership for Assessment of Readiness for College and Careers. 2011. *PARCC Model Content Frameworks: English Language Arts/Literacy Grades 3–11*. http://parcconline.org/resources/educator-resources/model-content-frameworks.

Plant, E. Ashby, K. Anders Ericsson, Len Hill, and Kia Asberg. 2005. "Why Study Time Does Not Predict Grade Point Average Across College Students: Implications of Deliberate Practice for Academic Performance." *Contemporary Educational Psychology* 30.

Rusch, Elizabeth. 2014. *The Next Wave: The Quest to Harness the Power of the Oceans*. New York: Houghton Mifflin Harcourt.

Webb, Norman. *Research Monograph Number 6: Criteria for Alignment of Expectations and Assessments on Mathematics and Science Education*. Washington, D.C.: CCSSO.

Williamson, G. L. 2006. "Student Readiness for Postsecondary Endeavors." American Educational Research Association (AERA). San Francisco: MetaMetrics, Inc.

Glossary of Reteaching Ideas

character profiles: Write key information about a character from the text onto a graphic organizer. Details might include age, gender, nationality, relationships to other characters (mother, brother, friend, enemy, or boss), physical characteristics, personality, strengths and weaknesses, and education.

character web: Write the character's name in a square in the middle of the paper. Draw ovals around the square with branches out to a series of ovals. Draw a line to connect each oval to the square. In the ovals, write words or phrases to describe the character.

For each activity marked with a computer icon, a template or graphic organizer is provided in the Digital Download. See the contents on pages 267–269.

connect two: In this game, two lists of words are posted. Players make connections between a word on the first list and a word on the second list, explaining the reason for the connection (e.g., synonyms, antonyms, or parts of speech).

concept maps: Graphic organizers are used to demonstrate and organize knowledge of a subject. The graphic begins with a concept enclosed in a box or circle. Branches are drawn from the box or circle, showing how the concept can be broken down into smaller parts, each with its own branches.

essential questions: Ask questions that dig down to the issues we struggle with or consider throughout our lives. They are not easily answered through a single text or exercise, such as "What defines life?", "Is art a matter of taste or skill?", "Can war be just?", "What makes a person a good friend?", or "How do we know what really happened?"

flip-flop: Rewrite or retell an existing story with a new tone (e.g., make something scary, funny; make something silly, sad).

Frayer cards: Divide a note card or piece of paper into fourths. Quadrant 1 houses a challenging vocabulary word. Quadrant 2 includes the definition. Quadrant 3 contains a picture of it. Quadrant 4 uses the word in a sentence. An alternative version integrates a synonym or antonym, too.

Freytag's Pyramid: Create a visual representation of a literary text's structure. Label a flat line at the bottom of the page *Exposition* or *Beginning*. Add a steeply angled line on the left, labeled *Rising Action*. Label the top *Climax* and the steep line down the right side *Falling Action*. Complete the pyramid with another flat line at the bottom labeled *Denouement* or *Resolution*. Add details from a current text to each part of the line.

Gimme 5: Write five key details from a text on a sheet of paper.

graphic organizers: Use visual shapes that help readers organize and analyze concepts and content from their reading.

inquiry charts: Gather information from several sources and compile it on a grid. Across the top, label the columns with topic-appropriate questions. Label the final two columns *Other Interesting Facts* and *New Questions*. Label each row with a separate source. Label the final row *Summary*. 🖥

newspaper headlines and story titles: Use headlines and titles to illuminate texts' main ideas.

personal dictionaries: These dictionaries contain vocabulary terms. They can be subject specific or alphabetical, English only or bilingual, contain synonyms and antonyms.

plot skeletons: Create a bare-bones description of a literary text's plot. Use a graphic organizer shaped like a skeleton, identifying the main character, his or her needs (obvious and/or hidden) causes, resulting complications, how these inform the decision that is made, and the resolution. 🖥

signal terms: Use or create lists of signal words to denote various text structures, such as chronological order, cause/effect, description, compare/contrast, and problem/solution.

Somebody Wanted But So Then (SWBST): Use this framework for creating summaries that is completed during reading. Write a summary sentence from the accumulated information.

song lyrics: Use song lyrics to provide accessible sources of figurative language.

storyboards: Create a series of images that depict the elements of a text.

story maps: Use these graphic representations to record and organize key information about a text. Typically, story maps include sections for information about the setting, characters, problem and solution. Sometimes, other information such as sequence of events, title, author, and main idea are included. 🖥

story summary graphic organizers: These graphic organizers provide visual spaces to record key information needed to summarize a text. 🖥

task cards: Create reusable cards containing one activity or question per card, breaking down a potentially overwhelming task into manageable pieces.

T-chart: Draw a two-column chart that enables readers to make comparisons, such as between words, characters, or concepts. 🖥

text feature BINGO: Fill in squares with various text features to reinforce concepts. 🖥

text feature checklist: Use a checklist as a student-friendly way to search texts to find text features. 🖥

Visual Thinking Strategies (VTS): Use a set of art-based techniques that use open-ended questions, neutral paraphrasing, requests for evidence, and linking of participant observations to help participants develop observational and analytic skills.

vocabulary matrices: Write one set of vocabulary words across the top of a grid and another down the first column. For each place where the row of one word intersects the column of another, write a sentence that correctly uses both words.

word associations: Lead a discussion about how words are connected, such as synonyms vs antonyms or examples vs. non-examples.

word maps: Draw graphic representations that connect vocabulary words to other concepts in various ways and include developing a definition, synonyms, antonyms, and a picture for a particular vocabulary word.

word sorts: Write categorized words on card stock, such as negatively connotative words versus positively connotative words.

words in context: Highlight surrounding words that provide clues to the meaning of unknown words.

The following documents are designed to help with the planning and implementation of close reading lessons. They are described in detail in Section One, Section Two, Section Three, and Section Four.

Page Number	Title	Filename
18	Incorporating Close Reading	incorporatingclosereading.pdf
51, 75	Planning Close Reading	planningclosereading.pdf
58–59	Annotation Ideas	annotationideas.pdf
63	Teaching Close Reading	teachingclosereading.pdf

Incorporating Close Reading

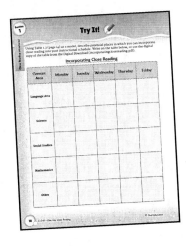

Planning Close Reading

Annotation Ideas

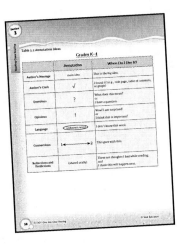

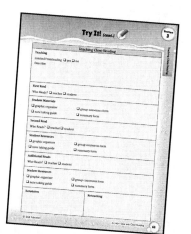

Teaching Close Reading

Contents of the Digital Download *(cont.)*

The following passages can be used to implement the sample lessons. See pages 77–259 for details.

Page Number	Title	Filename
82	The Ninja's Surprise	ninjassurprise.pdf
92	The Boy Who Loved Books	boywholovedbooks.pdf
102	It's About Time	itsabouttime.pdf
112	Bobbing Daisies	bobbingdaisies.pdf
122	Around the World in Forty Winks	fortywinks.pdf
132	Love Like Salt	lovelikesalt.pdf
142	How Colors Make Us Feel and The Color Game	colors.pdf
152	Al's Choice	alschoice.pdf
162	Alien in the Basement	alienbasement.pdf
176	Playing It Safe	playingitsafe.pdf
186	On the Wire	onthewire.pdf
196	Flying into Adventure	adventure.pdf
206	Drip, Drop, Down	dripdropdown.pdf
216	How Erasers Work	erasers.pdf
226	Bad Breath	badbreath.pdf
236	Too Cold for Trees!	toocold.pdf
246	Dear Mayor Keen and Dog Behavior	mayorkeendogbehavior.pdf
256	Playing It Safe and My Story	playingsafemystory.pdf

Contents of the Digital Download *(cont.)*

The following reteaching resources are designed to be used with the reteaching ideas listed in Appendix B (pages 264–266).

Page Number	Title	Filename
264	character profiles	characterprofiles.pdf
264	character web	characterweb.pdf
264	concept maps	conceptmaps.pdf
265	inquiry charts	inquirycharts.pdf
265	plot skeletons	plotskeletons.pdf
265	story maps	storymaps.pdf
265	story summary graphic organizers	storysummarygraphicorganizers.pdf
265	T-chart	tchart.pdf
265	text feature BINGO	textfeaturebingo.pdf
265	text feature checklist	textfeaturechecklist.pdf
266	vocabulary matrices	vocabularymatrices.pdf
266	word maps	wordmaps.pdf

Notes

Notes (cont.)